Table of Contents

The Orion Book (Volume 2)

Wes Penre

Book Two in the Series
Orion
Previous book in this series:
Book 1: *The Orion Book (Vol. 1) (2023)*
Other books by Wes Penre:
Non-fiction
Spiritual Handbook for the Twenty-First Century (2013)
Synthetic Super Intelligence and the Transmutation of Humankind: A Roadmap to the
Singularity and Beyond (2016)
Fiction
Fantasy Trilogy: "Ismaril's Journey"
The Book of Secrets (2021)
The Underworld (2022)

Wes Penre on the Internet

https://wespenre.com
https://wespenrevideos.com
https://wespenreboards.com
https://patreon.com/wespenre
https://ko-fi.com/wespenre

Acknowledgment

I want to dedicate this book to all my wonderful friends, patrons, and forum members who have supported me through the entire writing process. Your support has been a massive inspiration for me.

A special dedication to the Lady of Fire, who personally encouraged and aided me with such enthusiasm. You also know who you are. Your commitment is very much appreciated and has greatly helped me through the process of writing this book.

Foreword

This book is based on more than a decade of intense research but is at the same time a philosophical work. It's the second book in the series, "ORION." How many volumes will follow, if any, is currently unclear. New books will most likely follow upon this one, as I, and we as a collective, learn more. Therefore, I think it's important to read the books in the order I publish them to get the most out of my research. What I don't know, currently, is whether there will be more books in the ORION series, or if upcoming books will be standalones.

When we take a spiritual path, we start with an urge to do so (CARE, according to the eighth Hermetic Principle).[[1]] It has to do with focus.

Following this, we need to gain KNOWLEDGE (Gnosis in Greek) and research what is out there. We read, listen to videos, and we learn from others, incorporating what we consider has the most truth, and try to connect dots.

At one point, we inevitably must move into philosophy. Most of what we do before that is use our intellect, our left brain, to gather information and to process it; it's mostly an intellectual endeavor. But eventually, we need to move on and use the right brain, too, which has to do with intuition, imagination, cognition, personal insights, self-reflection, healing, and creation; thus, making a reconnection with Spirit that always surrounds us and travels through us at all time. Still, most of us don't pick it up; there is a disconnection from Spirit—a dissociation. Still, picking up on Spirit around us is every truth-seeker's goal, whether they are aware of it. It's the journey toward self-rediscovery: who we really are, where we came from, what we're doing here, and where we're heading. That's the entire purpose with truth-seeking in our Third Dimension.

When we have done our research, we go into ACTION. That doesn't always mean physical action, but spiritual action. The right brain has been severely suppressed in us all for ages because those in control of this world don't like philosophers; and they dislike critical thinkers. This makes the regulators lose control over humankind. It's shocking to hear Klaus Schwab, chairman of the World Economic Forum (WEF), saying that he will make sure all people who write on the Internet, or just read something on the Internet, that doesn't pass (the Elite controlled) fact-checkers as being scientifically correct should go to jail, even if the jails will be overpopulated[[2]]. He also said that in the future we will own nothing, and we will be happy[[3]]. Thirdly, he agrees with that we soon will live on eating bugs[[4]]. And it seems he is being heard. It's a significant chance these things will be implemented, and we are foretold. For one, this means the complete end of critical thinking and free speech.

School teaches us to conform
but the imagination teaches us to create.
Authorities [sic] teaches us to obey,
but curiosity teaches us to question.
Society teaches us to follow,
but the heart teaches us to lead.
The Path we seek is within,
do not be misled from without.
—*Gavin Nascimento*

Most of the world population uses very little of their right brain, which we might as well coin "the philosophical brain." That's where creation takes place; it's the feminine aspect of us, and it needs to develop in both men and women for us to break free from this Matrix. That is where the real awakening happens. Although the brain is just a physical vehicle, and a circuit board used by the mind (literally), creative thoughts ignite the neurons in the right hemisphere, which we use when we philosophize.

Therefore, eventually, the true journeyman will enter the infinite realm of philosophy, which awakes the creative side of the human mind (the Higher Mind, i.e., Spirit)—not to be confused with soul, discussed in The Orion Book Volume 1. As the reader will discover when studying this book, we are already creators, but our abilities have been suppressed by those who do not wish us the best.

With that being said, I hope the reader will have an interesting journey while reading this book. And above all, I hope it will help to bring on the philosophical aspect in the reader. If there is something this world needs more of, it's philosophers and freethinkers who dare to think for themselves; even when oppressive forces work hard to silence them.

Important to point out: Don't feel intimidated by the word *philosopher*. We can all be philosophers by pondering over what we learn about this reality and the vast universe beyond our extremely limited five senses; and we may discuss our thoughts and insights with like-minded wherever we find them. Thus, we can all help each other by creating a safe environment where we can expand our awareness.

Life is so much more than what we see with our physical eyes, hear with our physical ears, smell, touch, and taste. This is a matrix of death, and life begins *beyond* the limited five senses; so, let's explore life as it was meant to be. Let us explore how we can return to our natural state of being—for real. Let us connect the plug!

Happy Reading!

1: Terrestrials and Extraterrestrials of the Matrix

As expected, there are many kinds of beings living in this Matrix, whether they reside on or in what we perceive as *Earth* or in the astral dimensions. From a human 3-D perspective, we tend to distinguish between the following types of terrestrials and extraterrestrials, imagining them differing greatly from us, which is not true for the most part. If we narrow it down, we have six basic kinds of beings here, as far as my research is concerned.

The Different Astral- and Earthbound Beings

1. **Type 1: Soul-mind-spirit body (true humans).** In the *Wes Penre Papers* (WPP)[5], I called the original version of us humans the Namlú'u, but in this ORION series, it is more suitable to call humans in spirit form, and without our physical bodies, 3-UCs, which stands for "3-Unit Composite." This means that we humans comprise three parts in one: *soul, mind,* and *spirit body* (not to be confused with the sapiens body). For us to be human, we must inhabit all these three parts, or we are not considered human. We, as 3-UCs, were born in the Spirit Universe, also called the KHAA, Cosmic Water, Dark Energy, and ether (the Fifth Element). Sophia, the Creatrix of the Orion Universe, created the human soul group to comprise a spirit body, something previously unheard of. Humans are apparently the only species in the Universe having this privilege. Being creator gods from the get-go, we don't need to "earn spirit," like other star races do. The Mother Goddess, the Queen of the Stars, equipped us with vivid imagination and "godlike" creative abilities. We are the Queen's children. We are "mini versions" of her, naturally inhabiting curiosity, empathy, compassion, a wide range of emotions, and an ability to manifest our thoughts. We can manifest them even here in the Matrix, but it is not instant, like it is in the KHAA, outside the Matrix. The Matrix is of a lower density, which

makes it very difficult to manifest our thoughts here; but we can still do it, although we think the source of our manifestations might be something exterior from us. Little do we understand we are the true creators. However, we must realize we have been so manipulated and traumatized here that many humans have forgotten how to create, and most don't know who they are. Therefore, it can sometimes be very challenging to distinguish between a 3-UC and other star beings who roam the Earth. Some say that Earth is a school, and although it's tough and traumatic here, *we learn a lot and evolve through pain and trauma.* This is "En.ki talk" and it's not true. What we are told we can learn here, we already knew before we were lured into the Matrix and given amnesia. So, there is no justification whatsoever for letting us suffer here, and we very rarely learn something new. This is a matrix of control, it's a soul trap, and the prison guards, the Overlords, are pulling the strings via the Global Elite and down in a hierarchal manner. The average human is at the bottom of the hierarchy.

2. **Type 2: Soul-minds.** These beings comprise soul and mind but lack Spirit or spirit body. Therefore, it is appropriate to call them the 2-UC from here on (soul and mind). Most of them evolved inside or upon planets and stars, but in their evolution, they realized they could better navigate the Greater Universe (the ARY.AN or ORION Universe) if they abandoned their bodies and left their home world, much like a larva that turns into a butterfly. The body becomes a burden, and the soul group moves on; something we humans should have done long ago. The Greater Universe is pure Spirit, and later in their evolution, these 2-UCs can learn how to use the surrounding Spirit to become "creator gods;" distributing feminine Spirit Energy (Spirit Fire) to create in the Universe[[6]]. Before they gain access to Spirit, they can only create from what is already created; and they can, of course, use technology in these cases. But they can't create with their minds, using Spirit and manifest their thoughts in the outside universe. Some 2-UCs dwell in the astral, and others incarnate on Earth, usually in human

bodies. Just like us, they are caught up in the reincarnation cycle. They are quite indistinguishable from the original humans, except they may fall short in curiosity, imagination, and the search for inner wisdom, which usually is a driving force amongst the original humans and soul-minds who earned Spirit (see Type 3 below).

3. **Type 3: Soul-minds who gained Spirit**. These are the same as Type 2, but somewhere in their evolution, they develop to a point where they earn Spirit to create, with and without the use of technology. They learn how to manifest their thoughts and their imagination into the surrounding universe; they become creator gods. Some of these dwell in the astral, while others incarnate on Earth, usually in human bodies, indistinguishable from the original human soul group. This group can appropriately be terms 2-UC+, where the [+] stands for gained spiritual creative abilities.

4. **Type 4: Non-Player Characters (NPCs)**. These beings are completely of the Matrix and created *within* the Matrix. To the average person, these beings may appear human, but most likely lack soul-minds, as we think of it. I would suggest they have an astral body, just like we do (and the astral body is always of the Matrix), but they don't have a Higher Self (a genuine soul-mind or a soul-mind-spirit framework) that can live outside the Matrix. Their astral bodies are probably entirely programmed by the Overlords (in the WPP called *the AIF*) to fill certain functions. For the most part, these functions are used to distract us genuine beings from investigating things that matter, such as spiritual growth and inner development. I doubt an NPC will survive body death; instead, I would argue they dissolve and merge with the universal energy, losing the programmed personality they inhabited while incarnated on Earth (regarding dissolved and split souls, seen from a new angle, will be discussed later in this book). I would further suggest there are many more NPCs on Earth than there are genuine humans.

5. **Type 5: Artificial Intelligence.** Some might say Type 4 is also in this category, and they would be correct. Artificial Intelligence (A.I. or AI) is a broad concept and span from a cosmic magnitude all the way down to machine-like robots and androids possessing

some "intelligent" features. We all know that in today's world, the Global Elite and their minions are working around the clock to create AI that can duplicate and supersede human intelligence. New prototypes and revelations are made public in rapid progression, sometimes daily and weekly. The bodies they create for AI to operate in become more and more human-like. The purpose is to create human cyborgs (half biological and half machine), having eternal life (loosely speaking). Human 3-UCs will then host these bodies, so we can function inside a new Matrix, which now goes under the pilot term, "Metaverse." The overall agenda is also commonly termed "The Singularity." These cyborg bodies are already created, but we humans must be lured into this agenda step by step, so our minds get used to the New World Order.

6. **Type 6: The Invader Force (The Overlords).** These beings are the ultimate Control Force of the Matrix—the "Hidden Force." They mostly dwell in the lower astral realms, and they have artificial bodies being used when they travel through the Cosmic Water (space). Their soul-minds host such artificial bodies, created by technology. The Overlords lack Spirit and real creative abilities in general. They are indeed cyborgs (mind-souls stuck within a biotechnological body), and they are also miners, meaning they hollow out asteroids and planetoids and use them as spaceships within the solar system and, to some degree, beyond. There are reportedly a few of these Overlords on Earth currently. One such being is Marduk (Satan), and some others, inhabiting either human bodies that they have taken over by entity possession, or as in Marduk's case, he hosts regular human bodies like we do. He lives and dies here but can incarnate into a new body again quite immediately because he was born on Earth into a human body by a Sirian mother (Isis) and an Orion father (En.ki).[[7]] Regarding the rest of the Overlords (such as En.ki/Archangel Uriel/Lucifer), our density level doesn't match theirs, and they avoid incarnating here if they can avoid it. They rather possess chosen humans, such as the Global Elite.

The Seed Lines of the Gods

Now that we have covered the six different kinds of beings among us, it's time to break down the different human seed lines that have survived up to this day, but I will also cover the human main bloodline of the Second Construct (known as Atlantis, the time before Noah's Flood). Some of these bloodlines are kept reasonably intact up to this day, such as the Royals and other Global Elite seed lines (they marry within their own bloodlines), but the rest of us are a mix of all different lineages that have developed over the millennia.[[8]]

1. The homo sapiens seed line. These humans were the homo sapiens that existed before the Flood but went extinct in the Deluge (save for Noah and his family), so homo sapiens is supposedly non-existent, although there is some information, true or not, saying a few have survived underground, where they might still live if the rumors are true. The Third Construct became what we call the Matrix with a Grid around it. Here, En.ki created homo sapiens sapiens, which is "the thinking man," which is us. We are a downgrade of homo sapiens, specifically created to exist in this much denser construct. Hence, we are generally sturdier and stockier. Our DNA is tampered with so we can only perceive 4% of the Universe, while homo sapiens of the Atlantic Era in the Second Construct lived much longer (see the Bible, for example) and were more multidimensional.

2. The Lucifer-Isis seed line. This bloodline was the original *Elite* bloodline, which En.ki created before the Deluge; they are his human minions whom he initiated into his Mystery Schools and secret societies, such as the Brotherhood of the Snake. These Minions became Lucifer's High Priests (now the Global Elite). However, this bloodline was swept away with the Flood, but even after the Deluge, Lucifer and Isis continued creating this bloodline for a while, until En.ki was castrated by his brother, Prince En.lil[[9]]. This bloodline exists up to this day, and those who belong to it consider themselves of a higher rank than those of the other two bloodlines mentioned below. The "Lucifer-Isis seed line" is sometimes called *The Luciferian Elite Bloodline*.

3. The Marduk-Isis seed line. After Ninurta castrated En.ki[[10]], he let his son, Marduk (the biblical Satan), take over the breeding business.

Thus, Marduk "married" (read *raped*) Isis, and they physically seeded *the First Satanic Elite Bloodline*, until Isis managed to flee. She then created her own seed line (see "The Isis seed line" below) in honor of her "father," Prince En.lil. After that, she escaped to who knows where. Since then, no one has been able to trace her.

4. The Marduk-Ereškigal seed line. Shortly after Isis escaped, Ereškigal, the Queen of the Underworld, took over and helped Marduk seed another Elite bloodline. Contrary to Isis, she was eager. This is the main Elite bloodline in today's world and is *the Second Satanic Elite Bloodline.*

5. The Isis seed line. This is the bloodline Isis created after fleeing from En.ki. This seed line was conceived at Lake Baikal in honor of her "father," Prince Ninurta. Today, descendants of this bloodline are for the most part the red-haired, fair-skinned people. The red hair is from the genes of Isis. Most of those humans now reside in Ireland and the British Isles.

Note that seed lines 2-5 still exist in the 21st Century, so let us inspect from where these bloodlines originate.

The Lucifer-Isis seed line. This bloodline, in this Third Construct, began with Ham, son of Noah, forefather of the Southern Peoples (Hamatic north/northeast Africa descendants)[[11]].

The Marduk-Isis seed line. This lineage originated with Shem, another son of Noah, forefather of the Middle Peoples (of Semitic Asian and Arabian descents)[[12]].

The Marduk-Ereškigal seed line. Here we have the Japheth bloodline, and Japheth was the forefather of the Northern People (Japhetic Eurasian)[[13]].

The Isis seed line. As mentioned, these are the red heads, mostly represented on the British isles, but in particular, they are the Irish people.

So, the first three seed lines mentioned above originate with Noah's sons, and ultimately with Noah himself, who carried the "pure genes of En.ki." So En.ki, Marduk, Isis, and Ereškigal mixed their own genes by having actual sex, but then also added the genes of the three brothers in the mix to develop distinct human Elite bloodlines. All this genetic tampering happened in a rapid sequence. Ninurta (Prince En.lil) castrated En.ki in the Rigel star system at the beginning of this construct[[14]], so Marduk immediately took over En.ki's and Isis' genetic project. The assault on Isis was the main reason Ninurta castrated En.ki. Ninurta considered Isis being his "daughter," having been viciously used and abused by his stepbrother, En.ki. When En.ki could no longer procreate, Marduk immediately took over, until Isis fled the abuse, and Ereškigal finished the project.

I would argue that the reason for all this genetic tinkering was to create a human species that could better adapt to the decreased density of this Third Dimension, but it also had to do with ownership to some degree, establishing which god or goddess were in possession of which human bloodline. Noah and his sons were survivors from Atlantis and were not homo sapiens sapiens but homo sapiens. We can perhaps imagine they had a difficult time adjusting to this construct, so En.ki, and later Marduk, created new races; and because of the circumstances mentioned above, humankind at that point became three main root races. However, the three races might potentially have been planned already to begin with.

2: The Beginnings

At the Dawn of Creation There was Pure Spirit

In "The ORION Book" Vol. 1, I spent a long time discussing human history from before our 3-UCs were born and up to present time. So, if the reader wants a more complete history, I must refer to Volume 1. The following are updates and an expansion on what I wrote in the previous book.

Before I started writing this book, I went through a lot of material; some of it I knew since earlier, some of it I knew but now have gained more insights from, and some I had forgotten about. Still, there is material that is not yet sorted and connected. I continuously find interesting things that make me understand a little more, things I want to share. A part of it is about our history.

As an overview, Sophia, the Queen, created us humans as mini copies of herself, we could say. She as an Aeon (Spirit)[15], originating beyond this universe, in the so-called Pleroma.[16] Simultaneously, she also exists within it because the Orion Universe, her creation, is essentially Spirit, which is *her* Spirit, and thus, *her* imagination.

Sophia Manifests Within her own Creation

Sophia, the Spirit, the Aeon, manifested in her own creation—Orion. To distinguish herself from the VOID, she needed a "vehicle," an Avatar, so she also could move around in the Universe. She organized her Spirit Fires into a "unit;" almost like a spaceship she could travel in, metaphorically speaking; and this became Sophia's soul, which is the equivalent to the Avatar, what we usually call soul fire, but in truth is spirit fire, grouped together to form a unit—the soul. When Sophia attached the soul to her beingness, she became who we call *The Orion Queen, The Queen of the Stars,* or *The Mother Goddess.* There are many other names and titles for her in different cultures and in Orion.

Let us say she now had two choices. She could either continue creating in solitude to expand on her inner knowledge and wisdom as a Creatrix—a lonely and one-sided experience, I would presume—or she could split the spirit fires, which science calls "dark energy," (the KHAA/the ether) into innumerous smaller units. By giving these units lesser knowledge, she could see what they would create individually, but still being a part of Creatrix, their Cosmic Mother. She could thus create more ignorant units of consciousness from the ether and form individual soul-minds, using the four basic elements of existence to do so. These soul-minds could then be grouped together to form Avatars, making for an existence with lesser consciousness, initially. These Avatars work both as vehicles to travel the Universe and as memory containers and personality formations for a sentient being in the Orion Universe. Then, from evolution, a more developed Avatar would emerge, unique by its own experiences in an exclusive environment.

The Creation of Other Lifeforms

Thus, the Queen slowed down the vibration of spiritual energy in the KHAA/ether and created solid form, which we call matter. Stars, planets, nebulae, and galaxies came into being, on and in which these soul groups could exist. Then the Queen gave portions of her fire to the members of all the soul groups in different worlds, so they could develop in the physical (material) Universe.

To make everything more productive and creative, each world had a different rule set, flora, fauna, and environment. This was a way for the Queen to advance a universe where countless individuals could create with freewill, and she wished to see what would come out of that. It was all a huge experiment into the Great Unknown. The Queen could not expect what the outcome would be, which was the whole idea with the Orion Experiment. She wanted to learn from experience.

On the Concept of Soul Fire, Loan, and Payback

Those who are familiar with my work from the Wes Penre Papers, my blog, and the first Orion book also know that each Avatar comprises trillions of fires, making up our soul, as explained above. However, you might ask yourself, are these fires soul fires or spirit fires? I have commonly used the term "soul fire," which in the bigger scheme of things may be a little vague. It's true our real Avatars (with a capital "A") are made up of soul fires (fires of the soul/Avatar), but soul fires and spirit fires are the same. They have been described as bioelectricity, which is exactly what they are, but where does that come from? It comes from the KHAA—the Spirit Universe. If we want to be more correct (which we do), we should rather call them spirit fires than soul fires.

So, does everybody—even those on and in other worlds—possess Spirit to begin with, contrary to what has been claimed before? Yes, and no! Keep in mind that matter is Spirit in condensed form, and "ETs," who develop in different worlds as "newborns," possess spirit fire, which they have borrowed from Sophia to use for creative purposes to expand the Universe.

First, while developing in the physical worlds, beings sparsely contribute to the expansion of the Universe outside their own developing world. Most of their borrowed energy goes to maintaining their closed construct (a star, a planet, or wherever their evolutionary location might be). This is as it should, but at some stage in their development, Avatars usually want to explore what is beyond their construct because they have Sophia's curiosity and thirst for Wisdom (the two fundamental traits of Sophia, the Aeon). Therefore, star beings eventually might want to leave their world and explore the vast universe. In the beginning, they may build spaceships and discover stargates and wormholes, through which they can travel from one location in the Universe to another. For a while, this works well, but it is a slow process to travel from A to B. However, star races usually come to a stage in their evolution when they realize that their physical bodies are a hindrance more than they are helpful. Therefore, they decide to drop their bodies, leave their home worlds, and become galactic citizens in Avatar form (with no physical bodies). Now they can shapeshift, and they can move around in the lower dimensions of the KHAA by using thought alone. Travel becomes instant with the speed of thought. When they leave their physical bodies behind, these star beings and star races have entered the Nanoverse[[17]], which is the KHAA, the Spirit Universe beyond the physical worlds. However, they have yet to achieve ultimate creative abilities.

As these star races evolve some more, they get access to additional dimensions because of changes in their vibration, and eventually, many reach a point when they can use the surrounding ether to become true "creator gods," i.e., they can now manifest their thoughts by instantly transferring their inner visions and imagination from their mind to the outside universe, where their creations can be shared with others in what appears to be in physical form for them. Their consciousness has reached a level where they are not only capable of participating in other creator gods' creations; they are now creator gods, too. At this stage, they can also be assigned solar systems, where they can create new star races and oversee them. This is mostly done with technology.

This is when such beings start "paying back" on the loan, i.e., the collateral, which is the spirit fires the Queen lent them. Up to that point, they have mainly kept their energy boosted by borrowing more fire from the Central Fire—the wealthy spiritual energy source at the Galactic Centers (in our case, the Milky Way Galaxy). This energy has, up to that point, mainly been used to maintain the developing star beings' own existence, and their contribution to creation has been relatively low compared to the quantity they have used up for their own benefit, and that of their developing world. They would then eventually break even, and ultimately create on a grander scale and thus contribute to the expansion of the entire Universe. "Breaking even" is when the loan is paid in full, and the rest, after that, is "profit." I am sorry if this sounds like a petty Earth finance lesson, but it works as a suitable metaphor.

In the beginning, it took a long time before the first star race "cracked the egg" to explore the surrounding Universe. By now, many star races have done so, and there are many creator gods who create their own worlds and solar systems, and some even create galaxies and become Overseers of either star systems or galaxies. Thus, the Universe expands, and star races gain knowledge and can inflate. From there, Sophia grows in wisdom, and so does Source (the Monad, aka All That Is, First Source, etc.). Everybody wins through individual experiments, experiences, and contributions.

Warlike Star Races in the KHAA

Not everything went as expected because there are star races who become warlike in the developing worlds, and they may take their belligerent traits with them into the KHAA when they leave their home worlds. These beings rarely reach true creator god status because they never get access to the higher frequencies/dimensions, where they can use surrounding ether in their creative processes.

This has become a problem in the KHAA, and wars break out here and there, affecting the energy of the Universe negatively; expansion does not happen as rapidly as it was supposed to. Star races were not supposed to fight each other, but to work side by side to expand knowledge, and thus, the Universe. There have been (and still are) setbacks (the human soul group has become one such setback). Star races conquered other star races and created their own empires. An example is the Sirian Empire, discussed in the Wes Penre Papers. This empire developed into the Sirian Alliance when other warlike star races joined them. And after they had colonized other developing worlds, these were counted in as part of the "alliance," although star races in the occupied worlds were merely slaves to the intruders.

Why is it Called the Orion "Empire?"

There are readers of the Wes Penre Papers (WPP), who object to the term Orion Empire because it sounds so warlike. This is understandable. In fact, there is no "true" Orion Empire in the sense we think of empires, pertaining to conquest. There was once only Orion (no empire), but when the wars broke out, and star races created their own empires, Orion automatically became viewed as an empire, too, because anything warlike star races have not yet occupied is considered Orion. Thus, Orion became known as the Orion Empire by many star races, being one of many other empires.

3: Tiamat—The First Construct

Sophia's Choice

The Queen was not happy with how the Universe developed. Not all developing star races became warlike, of course, but there were enough to create chaos in some regions of Orion. Also, the more the wars took off, the fewer beings developed into true creator gods. It affected the overall expansion of the Universe, and something needed to be done.

This is when the Queen created a soul group that had full spiritual creative abilities from birth, instead of first evolve, then leave the home world, and eventually reach creator god status, which didn't always happen. Some races fell short because of their behavior. The Queen decided to create a world and a world environment in a higher dimension of the KHAA, beyond the physical universe and the developing worlds. Instead of using technology, which she had done when creating the developing worlds, she now created a new species and manifested this species directly in the KHAA—no technology needed. She created the human soul group. Then she equipped us with creator god status from the get-go. Our bodies were not made from technology (contrary to our sapiens bodies and bodies in other developing worlds) but were "dreamed up" by Sophia in her imagination, and then we manifested in the KHAA. Our bodies were immortal and comprised pure Spirit, and she gave our star race of her own spirit fire to make this happen. Therefore, we are a direct descendent of Sophia and the Queen of Orion, and we could say we humans are all "siblings." We are her children, mini versions of herself, inhabiting her traits. This is also why many star races in Orion call us "Royal." She wanted to know whether a star race, with full Spirit attached from the beginning, evolving on a relatively challenging world as "newborns," could develop without becoming warlike and hostile. She hoped we would develop spiritual attributes even in challenging situations, such as love, compassion, and empathy, which are important traits when we create as creator gods. If our soul group could do it, it might solve the war problem in the KHAA (in the WPP, I called us the Namlú'u, although I more often use the term 3-UCs in these Orion books[

[18]]). In addition, the Queen and her Helpers gave us full freewill with no strings attached to see how this would turn out. "No strings attached" means that if we humans in this experiment could graduate, we would not need to pay back the "debt." Our human souls are not supposed to be a loan—it's supposed to be a gift. However, the way things turned out, some adjustments to this needed to be made. More about that later.

The Queen also inserted a part of her own Spirit in Tiamat, the planet, so she could be close to her children. Our Mother was only a thought away, and we walked upon her "body" each moment of the day. Even now, part of the Queen's Fire remains at the core of the Earth but is also unfortunately being guarded by an Overlord Council, as told in The Emerald Tablets of Thoth[[19]].

If the Human Experiment showed to be successful, which in the beginning seemed to be the case, the Queen would implement this evolutionary experiment on all worlds from there on; and eventually, creation would become more constructive, and warlike races would be less likely to develop.

The Invader Force and Their Ferocious Captain

The Experiment went well, and Orion monitored it to study the progress. Then the Invaders came, as discussed in many of my writings (see The Orion Book Vol. 1 or The Wes Penre Papers, The Fourth Level of Learning[[20]] for a more detailed summary). In Greek mythology, this invasion is called "The Titanomachy"—the War of the Titans[[21]], also described in the "Enûma Eliš" (the Babylonian Creator Story)[[22]], and in other ancient texts.

There has been some confusion about En.ki's role in the invasion. Was he leading it, or was someone else in charge? I have found a comment from a reliable source that En.ki was already here in the solar system when Marduk and the rest of the Invaders attacked. He may not have planned the invasion, but was working with the Queen, the Vulcan creator gods (the men and women of fire), and his brother En.lil, although under En.lil's supervision, which he did not like at all, as discussed elsewhere. Thus, he already held resentment toward his mother, Khan En.lil, and his brother, Prince En.lil. Because of his engagement in the creation process, it is unclear whether En.ki was actually the brain behind the Invasion. He could still have been, only working in the background, pretending to be loyal to his mother.

In earlier writings, I confused Lucifer's Rebellion with the Titan War. I will go more into detail about this in the beginning of Chapter 5 in this book.

It was the Sirian wolfen-reptilian Marduk who became the Commander in Chief of the Invasion, even promoted to KHAN.US. KHAN.UR (Sirian King of Kings) by the rest of the rebels if he could utterly destroy Tiamat[[23]]. It was he who blew Tiamat into pieces and sucked out Mars' atmosphere in the process, where a second part of the Namlú'u Experiment was developing.

Marduk, the Sirian-Orion Villain

Marduk was the chief villain during the Invasion, and this is why Prince En.lil came to dislike him so much; more so than he disliked his brother, although En.ki began to shine in crime later. But at the time of the Invasion, En.ki had not committed any crimes anybody knew of. Still, if we think En.ki is bad, Marduk is ten times worse and has unfortunately since then put himself in charge here on Earth.

But who is this dreaded Marduk? Let's see if we can get some additional insight for better understanding.

If we read ancient texts and the translations and interpretations of such, we learn that Marduk is the son of En.ki. According to my research and my sources, this is correct. Some of you may have researched the Egyptian story of Osiris, Isis, and Horus, which tells the story. Osiris is En.ki, and as we know, En.ki is originally from Orion. Isis is at least half Sirian, if not "full-blooded" Sirian. Both En.ki and Isis sometimes incarnated here on Earth together in the Second Construct, and when Isis, in human form, got pregnant, Marduk's Avatar overtook the body as Horus the Younger. Hence, Marduk is half Orion (ARY.AN) and half Sirian, genetically speaking, born here on Earth in the flesh. This doesn't mean Marduk did not exist until he became Horus. He, as an Avatar, existed long before that. After all, he was the destroyer of Tiamat (Shiva the Destroyer) before Earth even existed. Whether it was intentionally done by Isis and En.ki to let Marduk incarnate is up for debate, or if Marduk simply took the body of Horus the Younger by force. Representatives from Orion also incarnated in the Second Construct to oversee En.ki's project, and they would not have accepted Marduk. Marduk has been here ever since, incarnating in different bodies over and over, just like we do, but of course, without amnesia. It is quite possible that he has incarnated into his own Orion-Sirian bloodline repeatedly, by taking the bodies of his own grandchildren or great grandchildren. He is here on Earth today, and if En.ki is Lucifer, Marduk is Satan, the "Lord of this World," as he is called by Christians. This leads to the question why Orion didn't capture Marduk when he was incarnated here and why they didn't bring him to justice for the hideous crime he committed when destroying Tiamat. I have not yet found a clear motive for that in my research material, but there are still much material to go through, and even more that I currently don't have access to, but hopefully will soon. One explanation could be that the agreement over who owns our solar system is still under debate between Sirius and Orion. The Khan Kings probably insist that they had the right to take back what was theirs, and that the Queen and her team are the invaders, not the Sirians. This brings us to the next question:

Why did the Sirians Invade the Solar System?

The real reason the Sirians invaded had nothing to do with Lucifer's Rebellion, as just mentioned. In fact, by the time of the Peace Agreement between Sirius and Orion, which happened long before the Queen created Tiamat, and which led to the "business marriage" between the Queen and Khan En.lil, the Queen showed the Sirians her goodwill and gave them a few sectors of the Milky Way Galaxy, which would be theirs to behold and create in. However, there was a caveat: The Queen required to be allowed to put her own "daughters" as overseers of these sectors to ensure the Peace Agreement was being kept.

So, when the Queen and her team of creator gods and overseers had created Tiamat and the human spirit group[[24]], a few Sirians noticed there were beings walking around on Tiamat (these beings were of course us, the Namlú'u). And they said to each other, "What are these beings doing on *our* planet?" The Sirians believed our solar system belonged to them as part of the Peace Agreement. There was a big argument about this, which might continue up to this day, and the Orion Council firmly stated that the Saturn solar system did not belong to the Sirians.

The fact that Orion refused to move their experiment greatly upset the Khan Kings, so they decided to "take back" the solar system they perceived was stolen from them, so they destroyed the planets on which the Experiment was ongoing, i.e., Tiamat and Mars. They didn't want to destroy the solar system, only the worlds which contained an experiment the Sirians had not given consent to, in their opinion. This was the real reason for the Invasion. Thus, there were no other star races involved in the Invasion than the Sirians, aka the Khan Kings.

Although Orion is confident that our solar system belongs to them, they need, per Orion justice, allow the Sirians access to the solar system, as well, until the dispute is settled. Therefore, in the Second Construct, there was a mix of Sirians and Orions walking about on Earth amongst the human spirit group.

In all this, the Saturn stargate remained closed on Sirian request. Saturn was our original sun (star), and when a stargate is closed, it means the sun is not sending energy into the solar system anymore, and no beings can travel through the stargate. So, they needed a new sun to substitute for Saturn. Because our solar system only had one enate sun (Saturn), a hub needed to be created, which is our current sun, most likely placed within Earth's atmosphere. This is not a real sun, just a "relay station." The Sirians, amid this conflict over ownership, apparently managed to negotiate that this hub, our sun, was going to take its energy from Sirius A, so the Sirians also had some influence over what they considered *their* solar system. Thus, our current sun is not what we see in the sky—it is Sirius A, whose energy is directed through our sun to shine over Earth and warm it up. Since then, our sun has also functioned as a direct stargate between our solar system and Sirius. In the Second Construct, this worked as a shortcut for the Khan Kings in our solar system, when they wanted to travel quickly between our system and Sirius.

When we learn that the stargate of Saturn, our original sun, was closed, it could also mean, on another level, when Tiamat was prospering, Saturn acted like a true sun in the KHAA (not in the physical universe, where it is a planet). But when Tiamat was destroyed, the entire Experiment fell through the dimensions, and to an observer, Saturn's light would turn off because its sunlight could not be perceived in the lower frequencies of the electromagnetic spectrum. Remember, the entire Experiment happened in the KHAA. For us, Saturn is just a planet because we can only see it from a 3-D perspective. Therefore, when En.ki formed Earth, he could not use Saturn because Saturn as a sun could not manifest as such in the physical universe, where Earth was created. Therefore, a new sun, created in the physical realm, must be used. However, there was no such object in the solar system, so he needed to use solar energy from elsewhere. I would suggest he used the solar energy from at least one star in Orion's Belt—perhaps all three. Then he created a hub, which is the sun we now see in the sky. Through this hub, the Orion solar energy can pass. Later, in the Third Construct (the Matrix), this energy was cut off, and instead, our artificial sun was connected to Sirius A with technology by the Sirians, as conveyed earlier. While directed toward Orion's Belt, our sun also worked as a stargate directly to that asterism. Now, it's a stargate leading to Sirius.

Hypothetically speaking, could it be that all the planets we see in the physical universe are suns in the KHAA, i.e., in the spiritual universe? Thus, there might be life on most of them, but not on this level/dimension of the Universe. Star races usually develop on stars or dwell inside stars (hence the term "star being" and "star race"). Perhaps, on a higher plane, all planets are suns, manifested by creator gods for their own creative purposes to be used by them. But in the lower dimensions, these stars manifest as "dead" planets. If this is correct, we will find very few planets with life on them in the physical universe. If we want to find life in the physical universe, we should primarily look at the stars and what (or *who* rather) is inside them. Planets, on this level, could potentially be used as storage or for mining.

However, in the Third Construct, the Matrix, our sun also became a "weapon" for the Sirians and for En.ki. With technology, they can manipulate our sun as they please, making it warmer and cooler, shoot out "solar flares," and create solar minimums and maximums, etc., and adjust the climate on Earth.

Moreover, when En.ki created the Matrix, he used Saturn as the "projector" for the holographic simulation we currently live in.

4: Earth—The Second Construct

The Fall into Matter

After the Invasion and the destruction of Tiamat, most of the Sirian Alliance who took part in the Invasion left the solar system, but some remained, and for a long time, the Human Experiment was dead. The Sirians let go of the Namlú'u who were in coma and were not able to escape together with Prince En.lil through the Saturn stargate before it closed.

It was now En.ki saw his chance to shine, but not yet in a criminal way. He wanted the Human Experiment to continue, he said. Tiamat was destroyed in the Spirit Realm, but bits and pieces of it had fallen into the physical dimensions and become solid. This is the asteroid belt we see today between Mars and Jupiter. So, En.ki, who was trained by the Queen as a geneticist, proposed that he should be in charge of creating new human bodies that would be fit for the physical realm, where he suggested the Human Experiment should continue.

After Tiamat, the Queen was determined to end the Human Experiment once and for all. It had failed, and she wanted everybody to come to her and go from there. However, there were star races who disagreed for there were many who put their faith in the human soul group. Most star races wanted a more peaceful universe with more compassionate creator gods. They said that we had done pretty well on Tiamat, and the Human Experiment went as planned and was very promising for the future. They thought we humans deserved another chance. Because the Queen was eager to make the experiment work, she listened to these star races, and she agreed that this was reasonable. So, she made a pact with En.ki and let him have it his way, so long as the Experiment went on. If En.ki could create functional human bodies with technology, the Experiment could continue. It was going to be more difficult for us humans now in this denser part of the Universe, and it would probably take longer for us to evolve, but time is not always an issue in the Greater Universe (Orion).

It could also be the case that those Namlú'u who fled with Prince En.lil through Saturn returned to complete the Experiment, so the entire Namlú'u group could graduate together. I have no reference to this; it's just a hypothesis, based on what I believe Orion wanted. The reason I believe this is, because the Namlú'u who escaped were still not ready to become full creator gods—they were not evolved enough—so Orion might consider it better if they, too, completed their progress in the new physical world, which later became Earth.

En.ki took a chunk of the exploded Tiamat that had descended and fallen into matter and created Earth, which was a much smaller "planet" than the gigantic water planet, Tiamat[[25]]. Because he was thoroughly trained by his mother, the Queen, in how to use Orion technology, he could create a construct that was much lower in density than our original planet. Although some 3-UCs escaped with Ninurta through the sun portal (Saturn) before the invasion was over, many of us went into a coma because of the shock. Remember, on Tiamat we were still very young 3-UCs in development. We were possibly like teenagers in our evolution when the invasion happened, and we knew nothing about war and violent conflicts. Hence, it was a shock for us, and the "RA Material," for example, channeled by Carla Rueckert in the early 1980s, tells us that after Maldek (Tiamat) exploded, we were in a coma for about 1,000 years[[26]].

When we woke up from this coma, En.ki was done creating Earth, and he had tried out different physical bodies, but had trouble making them work properly. From my discussion with certain sources, and by researching ancient texts, such as the Sumerian tablets, the Babylonian Creation Story, and the Gnostic texts, to name a few, I think we have a fairly good picture of what happened next.

En.ki Populates Earth

In the beginning, before the 3-UCs got invested in the new construct, En.ki created a prototype and then cloned these sexless bodies in the way he had learned from his mother. Still, he had problems getting human consciousness to stick to the inferior bodies he had created, but he succeeded eventually. Nonetheless, he had a hard time making us interested enough in his experiment to make us want to stick around. This was a lot harder than we remembered from Tiamat (we still did not have amnesia as we do now, and there was no Between Lives Area in the Second Construct. We had *some* amnesia, however, because of the denser existence in the material world). En.ki also wanted a solution to cloning, which took a lot of time and energy. So, he came up with the idea to split the human body into two genders, instead of being androgynous, as we were on Tiamat. At this time, En.ki introduced sex to the human spirit group. This was quite abnormal because usually, in other worlds, star races mostly procreate through cloning.

By creating this new human, he killed two birds with one stone. He solved the problem with having to create clones, but by making sex pleasurable, he got us interested in the experiment. He told us to try it, and of course, we liked it and wanted more of it. I think sex really hooked us already in the Second Construct, something the Pleiadians often claim in their lectures. Even some star beings outside the Construct are curious, wishing to come here and try it, and then immediately leave again. Of course, in the Matrix, we know that will not happen. They usually trap those who may enter the Construct, and they will recycle these souls together with us.

To begin with, we engaged in sex a lot, and we procreated and increased in numbers, and eventually, all humans, waiting in the astral for bodies, eventually got one. When we all became mentally invested in this construct, and our focus was much more on that than our true environment, we stayed on Earth, now more willing to work toward graduation. On Tiamat, in the KHAA, we could stay planetary, but in addition, we could also explore the cosmos outside the planet. In the beginning of the Earth experiment, we probably expected to do that again, and to some extent, we probably did. We had more flexibility than in this later Matrix, the Third Construct, and we could most likely move back and forth between Earth and the astral. Perhaps we were free to roam the entire solar system.

On Tiamat, we were androgynous—there were no genders, as we understand gender, and there was no death because we lived in the Spirit Universe, where death is non-existent. Now, with the Experiment brought down into the dense *physical* universe, death came upon us. However, at the beginning of the Second Construct, also called Atlantis, En.ki created bodies that could live for thousands of years.

Orion was never happy with En.ki's splicing into genders, and Prince En.lil eventually confronted him about it when he eventually came to Earth. But it was already done, so we humans continued hosting En.ki's sexual homo sapiens bodies. Sex for humans were pleasurable, and it made us procreate, which was the purpose, but sex soon also became a trap and a way to manipulate humans, and it's been used up to this day for this purpose. Now, in our present time, it's being used again to a large extent, just as it was at the dawn of Atlantis in the Second Construct. I am talking about Metaverse. As Prof. Sam Vaknin put it, and I paraphrase, "They want to create a society with no moral or ethical values, where everything goes. Then they want to put us in Metaverse while being in that condition. Already now, in Metaverse beta testing, people have already started raping each other's avatars. I'm horrified by humanity's future." It's interesting when mainstream academics are waking up, too.

En.ki's First Deal with Orion

The entire Second Construct is what we now loosely call Atlantis. After much brainstorming and by using trial and error, En.ki had created all these new bodies, and we were attached to them. Therefore, he had proven himself able to use Orion technology, being his mother's apprentice once upon a time, and he had created a workable experiment.

However, this deal, or agreement, came with a condition. Orion must have representatives on Earth to oversee the experiment, and even lead it. After all, it was the Mother's Experiment to begin with, not En.ki's. En.ki was not happy with this, but he had little choice. Still, he wanted the "new humans" for himself, considering us now being *his* creation. This increased his resentment that he might, to some degree, had overcome when he was creating homo sapiens, the inferior human. That was a way for him to shine.

The Orion primary stronghold on Earth became what is today's Egypt. This was not, however, the first Egypt in the history of our solar system. When Tiamat and Mars were populated with Namlú'u, Egypt was most likely located on Mars, and when Mars was nuked, and the experiment there destroyed, Egypt went down with it. But Orion reestablished Egypt on Earth at the beginning of the Atlantis era, sending Ninurta (Archangel Michael) as the Chief Observer to Earth.

The reason we can suspect Egypt was founded on Mars is because of the artifacts they have supposedly found there, such as alleged remnants of Egyptian sculptures, Ankhs, Egyptian statues, ruins, and more, spread over Mars' surface in certain areas. Researcher Billy Carson shared some of these pictures in one of his online videos, called, "Yes we went to the Moon, Yes we lied about it!"[[27]] Fascinating video in general. The reader can use their own discernment whether these pictures are genuine, but they seem to be, and they fit into the bigger story of our human past.

Although the original experiment was no longer, the Second Construct, at least to begin with, seems to have developed quite well. The density was of course much lower now than on Tiamat, but there were no major issues in the beginning, apparently, and En.ki continued working with the rest of the Orion team to help humans evolve with the purpose to eventually graduate. There were conflicts between En.ki and En.lil, but these conflicts seemed to work themselves out.

Because of the unresolved ownership issue over Earth, there were also Sirians here on Earth already in the Second Construct—both those who worked for Marduk during the Invasion and those who were still loyal to Orion, the so-called DAKH warriors, being part of the MIKH-MAKH army. All these Sirians were here in human bodies, and we often see them depicted in ancient texts with animal heads, implying they were "gods" in human garments (bodies). These ETs did not look as depicted in the Sumerian tablets, of course. It was just the way the ancient artists depicted their traits and characters, such as dogs, cats, crocodiles, hyenas, lions, and so on. They compared the gods with what existed in the animal kingdom on Earth. There were also representatives of other star races here, working with the Orions.

However, there was *one* being that was not welcome on Earth, and that was Marduk. Prince Ninurta, and the other ARY.ANs that were here then, knew Marduk destroyed Tiamat. It seems to me that Ninurta, aka Prince En.lil, had a special horn on the side of Marduk for personal reasons, as well. After the original human spirit group was formed, the Queen gave the solar system to Ninurta as a gift. This means Ninurta was responsible for the safety of Tiamat and the solar system. When Marduk invaded and won the battle, it created a lot of resentment in Ninurta. Perhaps he felt he had failed to protect us, and he blamed Marduk for it. He was the name figure who definitely did not want Marduk on Earth.

I see no reason why En.ki wanted Marduk here, either, at this time, but Marduk had other plans because he was the leader of the Sirians and considered himself having the right to be here. After all, it was "his planet," according to his own conviction.

Marduk Becomes En.ki's "Son"

The cosmic "family tree" is complicated and does not resemble the family trees we rely on for human genealogy. In the Universe, the term "next of kin" rarely pertains to physical families, unless we discuss the developing worlds, where it could be relevant. Therefore, when we relate Marduk to En.ki, saying he is En.ki's son, it is not exactly what we think it is.

Marduk, as a 2-UC, is a Sirian. When he invaded the solar system and destroyed Tiamat, there was, as we've discussed, no relation between him and En.ki. As we know, En.ki is from Orion, but there was also an important female player, a goddess, on Earth during the Second Construct, incarnating here. Some claim she might still be here. En.ki was infamous for being a heavy drinker of alcohol when he was on Earth, and he secretly slept with human women; but obviously he also had sex with ETs in human bodies, such as the Sirian-born Isis. He was also known as a seducer, and of course, a trickster. But so were Ishtar and Aphrodite, both alternative titles for Isis.

After En.ki and Isis had sex, she got pregnant and Marduk incarnated into that body as Horus. He is here up to this day, as discussed earlier, incarnated somewhere in a human body.

Ninurta and Marduk had many feuds between them during the Second Construct. We also know, because of ancient texts, that Marduk once tried to take Egypt by force and make himself King of Egypt. But the attempted coup was discovered, and Marduk fled and locked himself inside the Great Pyramid at Giza and escaped through a hidden door located inside the chamber where he took refuge.

The Chaotic End of the Second Construct

Because time here on Earth is considered linear, measuring time becomes quite difficult; particularly so the farther back in "time" we go. The time measuring systems will soon become inaccurate because time here is rather cyclic than linear, as discussed in The ORION Book Volume 1. According to how archaeology, and science in general, measure time, the Pyramids, the Sphinx, and more, are considered being constructs within this Matrix (the Third Construct), which is inaccurate. They are from the Second Construct, when Orion were here.

The same thing applies to many ancient texts, such as the Sumerian and Babylonian texts. Some, or many of them, may have been written (scribed) 5-7,000 years ago, but the cuneiform, for example, is often telling a more ancient history, dictated by the gods (often channeled and scribed by humans). A significant part of the texts refers to a time before the Flood, and time events are also mixed up because we must remember that the gods, who dictated the stories to the scribes, told these stories in a manner that suited them and made them look the way they wanted us to portray them. Therefore, many events, ascribed to have happened in the Matrix, happened in the Second Construct, such as the story of Isis and Osiris, and much more. The entire Atlantis Era, and that of Lemuria (MU) were of the Second Construct.

As the Atlantis Era progressed, and humans progressed with it, En.ki started experimenting with genetics again. He created many prototypes that he abandoned, letting them run free on the planet, where they created havoc. His fellow Sirians, and others, also incarnated here and raped and seduced human women, which is not in the least allowed. The children, who therefore had alien DNA mixed with humans, became the Nephilim, so often discussed—the giants of renown. Many of those became cannibals.

Suppose we try to analyze En.ki's psychological profile. In that case, we can see he is very impulsive, just like psychopaths often are. The reason for his out-of-mind experiments in genetics at the end of the Atlantic Era was probably because he wanted to show off again by creating better vehicles. I would argue that after the fallen angels had raped and contaminated the Experiment, En.ki tried to create new types of bodies to save "his" creation, but he messed it all up. He completely failed, which must have made him furious. And at the other end of things, Ninurta failed, too, because he had been given the solar system as a gift by the Mother to protect and keep secure, but because of the Invaders he failed to do so, and at the end of Atlantis, he failed to save the Experiment. He was probably furious at En.ki at that point. Well, it seems everybody was furious at everybody, which often is the consequence when mentally ill people, such as the Sirians, En.ki, and Marduk, operate.

To make a long story short, the entire Experiment turned sour and was heavily contaminated with En.ki's out-of-control play with genetics and the mix of ET and human DNA. The entire planet was a mess, and there was no longer any genuine progress here. Orion saw that there was no way to save the Experiment, so Khan En.lil decided to end it and call the human soul group home to Orion again. The plan was to flood the planet.

Some Words About Noah's Flood

There are those who have criticized Orion for instigating the Flood on us, and that is understandable. From what I hear, many think this was a betrayal on behalf of our Creators. However, there are a few things to keep in mind.

First, as we know from the WPP, Orion can't "save us," unless we come together as a spirit group and tell the Overlords or the Global Elite we've had enough. Then Orion can intervene because we don't have the resources to fight the Overlords. At that point, Orion will heed our call for help. That will make Orion act on our behalf because then they will operate under our freewill. As it stands now, in present time, it's difficult for them to intervene because the human soul group has showed no interest in putting an end to this construct. This is something that was also mentioned in the RA Material. For those outside the Matrix to intervene, there must be "a cry for help," and it must come from the group at large.

By the time of the Deluge, a similar thing must have happened. The human soul group was crying for help because their existence on Earth became unbearable.

Second, what the Flood did was to wipe out the homo sapiens bodies, i.e., En.ki's model, and we could return to our native state in the KHAA, without the physical connection to the material world. In that sense, we would evolve. Like "Jesus" said, we must cast off our garments (our physical bodies). Those who "worship" the physical body have no place in God's Kingdom. This was changed from Queendom to Kingdom, and from Queen to God, but otherwise, the concept is valid. To Orion, our physical bodies are an abomination because we are Spirit to begin with—we are not physical beings. We fell into matter when En.ki seduced us into these bodies through sex. If we had stayed on Tiamat, and the Sirians had left us alone, we would have graduated a long time ago.

Third, but not the least, and from what I've learned, the main reason for the Flood was the splicing of human DNA that occurred here. It seems clear now that although En.ki created homo sapiens in the Second Construct (or rather modified us), he did not add his own DNA into the mix by then. However, at the end of Atlantis, when En.ki and other non-humans mated with humans, a splicing of DNA took place, which is very illegal, and is frowned upon by the Orions for ethical reasons. What such a thing does is to contaminate the Experiment, and the purpose with the entire project turns sour. It's like if you create a bear to reach a certain goal that a bear can accomplish, someone comes and turns the bear into an armadillo. It is very difficult for an armadillo to accomplish the goal of a bear. This is a very rough analogy, but hopefully the reader gets the drift. The Experiment was destroyed by En.ki and other ETs—thus, the Flood. There was nothing here to save.

As we know (see Chapter 1 of this book), En.ki, Marduk, Isis, and Ereškigal practiced DNA splicing on several occasions in the beginning of the Third Construct (the Matrix), but then Orion could do very little because En.ki had set up the Grid to protect his new experiment from intrusion, and he kept us captured here in the "dark" with full amnesia.

The intention behind the Flood was to release us and let us ascend from the physical realm to Orion. Of course, we can argue whether a Flood would be the best way to accomplish that, and there are different opinions about it, most of them valid, but at the end of the day, if we were the Orions, how would we eradicate the physical bodies? It's an open question. Was a Flood maybe the quickest and easiest way, after all? Perhaps there was no pain-free way to go about it.

We know the rest of the story, pertaining to the Flood. En.ki tricked Orion by pretending to go along with the Flood, although he wanted his homo sapiens creation, "his" experiment, to continue. But he saved his pure bloodline, which was Noah's bloodline, and he also hijacked, or seduced, many humans to follow him. An "Ark" was built (which was actually an aircraft—a "spaceship"—where he put Noah and his family, and a group of humans (3-UCs) he wanted for a new experiment. We, who are currently living on Earth, and are trapped in this recycling process, are the humans En.ki gathered for this experiment. Still, there seems to be many 3-UCs who went back to Orion at that moment. We are just the remnant of a larger soul group that has now been dispersed, and we, who are in the Matrix, are the only ones left of the Human Experiment. The escaping 3-UCs are most likely creator gods in the KHAA by now.

The question is, did we go into this Matrix willingly, or were we "kidnapped?" I don't know the answer to that, but I have seen references to us being manipulated through sex again; perhaps by listening to En.ki's slick tongue once more. Others, who have remote viewed this event, say that it looks like the human 3-UCs were in deep sleep on "Noah's Ark." It's hard to say what is true, and I have no confirmative information on this.

5: The Matrix—The Third Construct

Lucifer's Rebellion—When it Happened Exactly!

I have discussed Lucifer's Rebellion a few times over the years, and although Lucifer's (En.ki's) actions are probably quite correct as described in the Fourth Level of Learning, Paper #5[[28]], I got one thing very wrong, and that is the time frame within which it happened. This must be corrected to tell the truest version of human history as possible.

During the "Wes Penre Sessions," between 2010-2015, the Rebellion was discussed with particularly one of my sources, who is from Orion. What was never mentioned, however, was the time frame, so that was for me to figure out. Not until I researched this book I came upon major hints as of when it occurred. The Rebellion did *not* happen before the Titan War, as I had presumed. *It happened after Noah's Flood and the destruction of the Second Construct.* It ensued when En.ki realized that he was not going to be in charge of the human soul group, and become the King of Earth, which he had planned, and this was just before Noah's Flood. Orion wanted to terminate the Experiment once and for all, and this is when En.ki rebelled, and it happened over a period of time, which will be explained here in the beginning of this chapter.

Understanding our history is a learning curve, and when we make mistakes, we need to correct them to come closer to the truth. In fact, we learn nothing new; we have known all this before, but we have forgotten. All we do is starting to remember...

Lake Baikal and the Artificial Soul

After the Flood, Orion considered the Human Experiment cancelled, but once again, this did not happen. Most 3-UCs probably went back to Orion after the Flood, but we who still reside here on Earth did not. We were captured by En.ki to be used in his very own Experiment, which he wanted to oversee without Orion's involvement. This time, he was going to be the King of Earth—finally.

By now, he was quite aggravated, and in his prideful way, he felt betrayed and mistrusted, because he had secretly considered the Second Construct Experiment his own. He was the creator of homo sapiens, so therefore, we are his children, from his perspective. Hence, he literally kidnapped us, and he even brought Isis into the new Construct he now created—the Third Construct—our construct, which we also call the Matrix. He also let the displeased Sirians and others into his construct to help him safeguard it, and most likely to build a counter army against the Orion MIKH-MAKH. He lowered the frequency of Earth, tilted it slightly, apparently put a protective physical Dome around the planet, and when he had incarnated the 3-UC here, he put up the Grid as an ultimate shield against outside interference, but also to prevent us to leave the construct. This Grid mainly comprises the collective human soul energy, so it was quite powerful in the beginning. Now it is weakened because the energy on this planet is being depleted. We will go into this some more later.

Because of the tilt, the Earth was now difficult to detect from outside, putting it within a very unusual frequency band. Moreover, he used Saturn as a projector of cosmic waves, ensuring that Earth kept itself stable within En.ki's desired frequency band.

Next, he created a new and denser human body, which would be sturdier and heavier, so it could function better in the frequency of "visible light," which is only 4% of the spectra of the Universe. He wanted to limit us and to make us forgetful, or he was afraid we would rebel. Knowing that we are very powerful when we show that side of ourselves, being spirited, he fears us and understands we need to be restrained to be controlled.

Therefore, he turned off about 96% of the DNA in our new physical bodies, the homo sapiens sapiens, ironically referred to as "The Thinking Man," when it's exactly the opposite. We went from "thinking" to "thinking less."

In the new construct, being much denser than the Second Construct, his human bodies had a much shorter lifespan, and everything here died quite rapidly. So, he set up the "Between Lives Area," the BLA, to recycle souls and give them full amnesia. This was the plan, and after some time, he knew how to accomplish it. He decided to create an artificial soul.

In the Nag Hammadi texts, we are told that En.ki (Yaldabaoth, aka the Demiurge) created an artificial soul and an artificial spirit. If we don't have the Bigger Picture, it is difficult to understand what these terms mean, but in this book, we are going to explore just that, among many other things. Important at this point in the story is to explain what the artificial soul is.

Following the procedure he had learned from his mother, he used the four elements and let the lightning strike into Lake Baikal in what is now southeastern Russia. Thus, he created soul fires that were of *his* construct, and they were therefore restricted to his construct, which includes the astral planes around us, within our Earth atmosphere, we could say. The souls were created on Earth, using the astral that runs through the atmosphere to do so. He then constructed his own avatars, which we now call the astral body. All this put together became a soul because he now had the fires he could organize into individual groups that create the avatar. Thus, the astral body became the artificial soul.

The Trickster God

Over and over in ancient texts, En.ki is called the "trickster god," and that is for a reason. First, he tricked Orion and created his very own experiment, stealing the Avatars from Orion's Experiment and calling us his property. Some say En.ki loves his "creation" (homo sapiens and homo sapiens sapiens), but that is only partially true. En.ki is selfish, prideful, narcissistic, and psychopathic, and it is becoming more and more obvious the more we dig into our history that to him, we are only tools and objects to fulfill *his* dreams (introjects) and goals. We know from ancient history, and from sources of mine, that En.ki and many other star races and star beings are jealous of us because we inhabit Spirit, and they don't. En.ki does not and has never understood Spirit. Ninurta understands it intellectually because he's been educated by the Mother Goddess, and with that Knowledge, he has an advantage over the rest of the Archangels and the Khans.

En.ki always knew he is mortal, and that one day he will cease to exist. Apparently, this has weighed on him, and he wants our immortality, i.e., our Spirit. And what is our Spirit? It's our original bodies—the Namlú'u. At one point, he realized that he needed our minds in order to conquer our

Spirit. It is impossible to say when and where his thoughts developed into this agenda, but I would guess it came to fruition by the end of Atlantis. This was something he obviously never mentioned to any of the Orions. He figured that if he could manipulate our minds to think like him, he could take us over and thus conquer our spirit bodies and by that become immortal and the King of Earth and over the human soul group for as long as it pleases him. If we study the ancient texts, such as "The Epic of Gilgamesh," it tells the story of Gilgamesh, the demi-god, who lived a very long life, but he wanted immortality. He searched for many years, but he never achieved it. The ancient history is full of similar stories, and now we're there again. This is what the Singularity is all about—immortality through technology. They make cyborgs of our current bodies by remodifying our DNA with nanotechnology, promising us we will live forever. We become like the gods because that's what *they* are—cyborgs.

So, at one point, En.ki started working his way toward the Singularity. Perhaps then he did not have the intention to invade Orion, only to take on our spirit bodies for his own immortality's sake, and for the sake of control.

We don't know if Orion, after the Flood, was aware there were survivors who were kidnapped by En.ki. Of course, they found out, eventually, but I can't say at which stage that happened. It seems like one of the first things En.ki did was to hide Earth by tilting it and putting it within a frequency where it was hard to find. Thus, he had time to create his new construct, free from interference.

Inserting 3-UCs Into the Matrix

According to the Pleiadians, and some other channeled material, it appears we got tricked into this Matrix through sex—again. I don't know how we could have been fooled again, but somehow, we must have been depleted of most of our memories. It could be he kept us captured in a lower frequency, where it was dense enough to prevent us from remembering. Then he used the sex trickery again and trapped our consciousness in his artificial avatar—the artificial soul, which he was in control over. Then we incarnated into the new homo sapiens sapiens bodies, which were extremely restricted and receptors of a hologram projected from Saturn, creating a simulation, which is our "3-D;" all created by Orion technology that was misused.

Lucifer Recruiting Allies Amongst the Rebels

En.ki could not do all this alone. That would make him very vulnerable—both to us and to Orion. Therefore, he went to Orion and started recruiting discontent Sirians, who were part of the Invasion, but also other star beings who wanted to rebel against Orion and take over the Universe. It seems very plausible that En.ki as Lucifer recruited his cohorts very carefully, and he explained his plan. At this time, I think he knew what he wanted: to go to war against Orion and become the King of the Universe. And he promised his cohorts immortality through us. I think this last sentence is the reason why so many followed him back to the Matrix to support him. Marduk was one of them. You can read the entire story about the Rebellion in "The Wes Penre Papers, The Fourth Level of Learning, Paper #5."

In conclusion, many star beings, mostly Sirians, followed En.ki back to Earth, and most of them have been here ever since.

More on Death and the Afterlife (the BLA)

After having created the astral body, the artificial soul, it was easy to trick the 3-UC ,whose body had died, to go into the tunnel of light, or wherever the Overlords wanted to direct them. In this avatar, the memory of the recent life is stored. When we are lured into the recycling center, we first get a life review. The BLA workers then emphasize the bad things we've done during our lifetime, and how those things must be corrected and the karma taken care of in the next life. Usually, the soul agrees, feeling bad about their behavior, whether true or not. However, by that time, the false avatar is slowly thinning out, and the soul does not remember the entirety of his or her past life anymore. So, the BLA worker also includes the Overlords' karma in the process, saying that this is what *the discarnate soul* did, and it needs to be taken care of. The deceased now thinks this is his or her karma when it is not. The deceased agrees to do his or her best to accomplish this next time around. By taking on *their* karma, we have a trauma bond with these beings, which they can use to take us over.

Then the artificial soul, the avatar, is destroyed, and with that, the entire personality we were in the previous life. No memories left, blank slate. Our previous personality is gone forever from our Matrix memory. The soul fires that En.ki created, making up the false avatar[[29]], are gathered and mixed with other soul fires from other dead humans and then stirred together, making up a new false avatar, i.e., artificial soul. Our 3-UC is then "glued" into this new avatar. Then, before being shot down into a new body on Earth, which usually is a body within the same bloodline as in the previous life, the new avatar is reminded of the karma. All this time, our 3-UCs are attached, first to the old avatar, and then transferred to the new avatar with the blank slate. After that, the new soul is shot down into the body of let's say his or her own grandchild, and he or she starts all over from scratch with amnesia and builds a completely new personality.

Why are they making it so complicated? Well, they must have our consent, and they get that during the life review. If we consent to going back to Earth, they can destroy our avatar, mix soul fires, and with that erase the last of our memories, create a new soul with a blank slate, and shoot us back down with the captured consciousness of the 3-UC attached. *They need our consent!*

To me, this shows that En.ki has very little to no empathy, is perhaps the archetype for narcissism, and later, in his case, also turning into a psychopath, and ever since he was demoted before the Tiamat Experiment, he has been resentful and plotted for revenge. But when he was allowed to create the first homo sapiens, he might have put that on a shelf, pleased to be "number 1" again to show off for his cosmic family and other star beings who doubted his grandiosity—or so he thought in his introject. When the outer reality no longer corresponded with his introject, he went into a narcissistic rage and plotted for revenge, after which he created the Matrix[[30]].

The Orion Threat

Prince Ninurta figured out that En.ki had rebelled and had recruited a lot of people on his quest. So, he spoke to the Queen and Khan En.lil. The Khan became furious, and he assembled the MIKH-MAKH, and he and Ninurta started a war against the rebels in our solar system. Ninurta also required that En.ki set his daughter, Isis, free. En.ki refused.

Eventually, the rebels realized that Orion was so much stronger, so they (probably En.ki or Marduk, or both) came up with a plan to cooperate with Orion. A contract was "signed" between them. If Orion agreed, En.ki promised to let the humans evolve and go back to Orion, just as the plan was in the beginning, when Tiamat still existed. If Orion would not agree, both Isis and humanity would be in "danger," i.e., the rebels would destroy them. Of course, as spirited beings, we are immortal, but the soul-mind we use in Orion is not necessarily so.

Thus, a contract was made, although it seems that in retrospect, En.ki and his team had no intention to fulfill it. For them, the benefit of a contract was that it gave them plenty of time to set up what we now know as the Singularity. The Overlords first had to let us "evolve" enough to be ready to take on the Singularity, and the Rebels must manipulate us to such a degree that they could take over our minds and ride our Avatars in a direct attack against Orion.

The trickster god had an advantage before Orion because he had us as his hostages and could therefore do most of the bidding. He could, of course, just have told Orion to leave him alone, or he would destroy us humans. However, he probably thought it to be better if Orion did not breathe in his neck. If an agreement was made, it would be easier to accomplish his hidden goal in peace.

The Castration of En.ki

In the WPP, Level 4, I discussed the Rigel War. The Sirians, and others who rebelled with En.ki had access to outposts in other star systems because of previous conquests and the gift from the Mother through the Peace Agreement, and although these rebels were not spirited, they could travel through stargates in their hollowed-out crafts, and they most likely used the sun stargate to first navigate to Sirius A and continue from there to the next hub.

Then En.ki and other rebels started a devastating conquest war in the Rigel System, in which the MIKH-MAKH got involved in a counterattack. But during that war, Prince Ninurta became aware that En.ki had raped Isis to create a new bloodline, and that she had fled and could not be found. Ninurta went furious and castrated En.ki. Whether he did this literally, I don't know, but let's say he made En.ki "impotent," which has sexual overtones, of course, but can have a greater meaning: We may use the term impotent when someone is incapable of doing something, for example, losing the creative abilities.

What I know is that this is the time when Ninurta as Archangel Michael cast En.ki and the rebels out of Orion, and they became the "fallen angels," as told in the Bible and elsewhere. Ninurta threw En.ki into the Abyss and "chained him" there. Both En.ki and the rest of the fallen angels were stripped of their creative abilities, and they could not even move around by themselves anymore. They could not even take bodies.

In some manner, these beings managed to create artificial bodies, cyborgs, whom we today call the Greys. Many of these "Grey aliens" are Sirians occupying these bodies, being half machines, resilient to the harsh conditions in space/the Cosmic Water. Thus, they can still move around, but their realm, from where they now operate, is lower in frequency than ours. In fact, it's the lowest regions of the astral—the astral being an intermediary between the physical and the spiritual. I had it explained to me that the astral in general is a very low density of the Greater Universe. That's the Abyss, or the "lower five heavens" in some ancient texts, also sometimes called the Hell Dimensions. And in the deepest region, En.ki is trapped. The Khan Kings travel within the solar system, and sometimes to some of their occupied worlds, including the worlds the Queen granted them, using solid asteroids in the process, but we usually can't see them because they operate in a lower dimension. Sometimes, they shapeshift into our reality, or they accidentally get into our atmosphere and crash land (think "The Roswell Incident," for example). It's not that they can't come in here, but they rather not, because here they age more quickly, and that magnifies their anxiety about mortality.

Instead, Marduk, the Global Elite, and especially we humans, as a whole, are helping En.ki on his quest, unbeknownst to most.

Since the fallen angels were stripped of their creative abilities, they have been completely dependent upon us. Many talk about the Overlords being addicted to gold, and they take it because it will help them age slower. But what are they really talking about? Are they actually inhaling gold or is it our spiritual energy that is the "gold," and gold is the same as loosh? I would say so. They need our energy to survive, or they will run out of energy completely, just like any narcissist would here on Earth.

Marduk Becomes The Prince of Darkness

The only two or three of the Rebels I know of who can still move around freely here on Earth are Marduk and Isis, and possibly Ereškigal because they were and are incarnated here on Earth and were not affected by the fall of the other angels. I exclude Isis from this list because she is missing. The other Overlords, who must use machine bodies to move around, sometimes visited here on occasion, when absolutely necessary, but they did not stay long because of the aging issue. According to the Sumerian texts, 2024 BC was the year when the gods left Earth "for good" because they aged rapidly. That means Earth was left to Marduk, which I'm sure he didn't mind at all. Now, he could control humankind from Ground Zero, while his "father" had to do the manipulation of mankind remotely. This created a chasm between En.ki and Marduk, where both wanted to be in control over the other. This conflict has continued ever since, and this is part of why we see so much turmoil, so many wars, and so much insanity that does not make sense. I will go into this a lot more later in this book.

The Reset

What has just been discussed is about what happened shortly after En.ki created the Matrix. The Flood swept across the Earth about 9,600 years ago, and that is how long the Matrix has existed, and we are of course still in it. But nothing is forever, and we are very close to a reset, when we go from Marduk's age, The Age of Pisces, to En.ki's age, which is The Age of

Aquarius. The Great Reset will happen when the Singularity is in place, in my opinion. But even though the upcoming age is supposed to be En.ki's, there are no guarantees. The gods always fight over dominion, and dominion over the Ages, and the strongest wins, and the opponent will often be destroyed (killed). This is Sirian mentality, and Marduk, being Sirian, is certainly of this mindset. When the Singularity is coming, the two opponents, who sometimes work together, and sometimes fight, will battle it out. In Marduk's mind, there is only space for one of them, and that is the winner. If he defeats En.ki and takes over the human soul group, and the attack on Orion will actually take place, there is no room for En.ki. He will most likely be either left behind or killed. I believe En.ki has the same mindset—he *must* have because he would never be able to relax so long as Marduk is alive after a successful invasion. There can only be one King of Orion.

6: On Spirit, Universes, and Things in Between

The Pleroma vs. the Universes

There are, of course, different "schools of learning," and I am presenting one of them. None of these schools (including mine) has all the answers. By using intuition, connecting dots, and including and excluding, and not the least—pondering deeply on the subjects—we get a growing picture of our current reality and what lies beyond.

In the "truth community," in lack of a better term, many are acquainted with the Gnostic texts, and the Nag Hammadi in particular, or they have at least heard about them. Although these texts promote a masculine Source (the Monad) and portray Sophia as the Aeon who made a mistake when she created matter (the physical Universe), which I consider erroneous, there are interesting parts in these texts worth studying. One such interesting part is the subject of the Pleroma.

The word *Pleroma* is a Greek word, and it means "fullness[[31]]."

[1]b: the fullness of being of the divine life held in Gnosticism to comprise the aeons as well as the uncreated monad or dyad from which they have proceeded.[[32]]

Further explained in the texts themselves, the Pleroma is also specified as "where" the emanations of the Monad, the Aeons, are spiritually manifested. These are creative emanations of the unfathomable Monad (masculine), each Aeon with its own unique major trait and characteristic, from which they create for the all-encompassing Monad to experience, so he may expand and learn more about Himself through individuated, "spliced" parts of Himself. Still, the Pleroma is not "outside" the Monad because there is no such thing. As mentioned, the Monad is unfathomable, and therefore, we must use our limited vocabulary to discuss these matters. It must be mentioned here, as well, that the Pleroma is pure Spirit—that is all it is, and the Aeons are pure Spirit, too, but perhaps a few times removed from the Monad.

According to the Nag Hammadi texts, Sophia is one of these Aeons, and her major trait or characteristic is Wisdom. This does not mean she is all-knowing and omni-wise because if she were, there would be no reason for her existence. When we say Sophia is Wisdom, it means she is constantly working on achieving it. To achieve Wisdom, she must be curious, which is one of her aspects. Does that not also define who we, the spirited humans, are? If you're reading this book, are you not reading it because you're curious and want to achieve more Wisdom? I've said it before: We are "mini copies" of Sophia.

We know next to nothing about what other Aeons are creating, but we know more about Sophia. It is because she is our Creatrix, and she created our specific Universe—Orion. But our Orion Universe is not the only universe Sophia has created so far. In the WPP, the Second Level of Learning, Paper 2, under the section, *A New Way of Looking at the Structure of the Omniverse from an Interdimensional Perspective*[[33]], I discuss this at length. Sophia's universes come in clusters of twelve, where she, the Aeon Sophia, is number 13. Orion is only one universe in a cluster of twelve. Then there are other clusters of twelve.

I have stated in my writings that the KHAA is the Spirit Universe. Alternatively, I have termed it the ether, Dark Energy, the VOID, and the Cosmic Water, to name a few—different names for the same thing—Spirit.

Then what is the difference between the Monad, the Pleroma, and the Orion Universe? It's the same and only Spirit, and if we incorporate the Gnostic terms, they all originate within the Monad. We could argue if the Monad is essentially Spirit or not because He is unfathomable, but it's easier, from a philosophical perspective, to consider Him Spirit, too. Either way, He emanated Spirit within Himself, and then emanated the Aeons, whom from thereon have created universes and everything therein.

Hence, the Orion Universe, the KHAA, is pure Spirit running through all creation. So, per definition, even those soul-minds who are not "spirited" still have Spirit running through them, although they can't pick it up; and their fires are spirit fire, although we call them "soul fires" when we discuss the physical, developing worlds. There is nothing in Creation that is not of Spirit. Everything that is created is made with Spirit Energy, although diluted to different degrees, depending on how much of it is used in a particular creation, and how condensed that creation is.

With all this in mind, what distinguishes Orion from anything and everything "outside" the Universe? Again, we must use terms we humans can understand how to communicate these highly metaphysical thoughts, so here we go. When having all this explained to me many years ago, metaphors were often used. All That Is, i.e., pure spiritual energy is like an endless ocean, constantly moving in wave patterns, much like an ocean here on Earth—but of course, much less dense.

When Sophia creates universes, she first creates a "pond" within this Great Ocean, and in this pond are water lilies. Each water lily is a universe. These lilies are then assembled into clusters of twelve, and on a distance from this cluster is another cluster of twelve universes, and on it goes. Thus, one of these water lilies is Orion. Each water lily in our reality has a roundish boundary (although I suggest a real universe is egg-shaped). Outside this boundary is the Endless Ocean (the Super-Cosmic Ocean). But the Endless Ocean also runs *through* the water lily, so the Cosmic Ocean is always present in everything. The Endless Ocean, the Cosmic Ocean, is the VOID or the KHAA. What Sophia did was to set up a boundary in the Cosmic Ocean, encompassing a certain "area" of the KHAA that she claimed was hers. Within that, she created Orion.

Pondering all this, we can see Sophia made no mistake. All she did was to create within these boundaries, making sure nothing created inside it could break this boundary. This is the reason I've said a few times over the years, what is created in *this* universe stays in this universe. We can't swap universes because these other universes have unique properties, and nothing in here could, in its current form, function elsewhere.

From within this vast area of pure Cosmic Spiritual Energy, Sophia created the developing worlds, the physical universe, i.e., the planets, the stars, the galaxies, and more. These worlds are not separate from the KHAA; they are just manifested creations *within* the KHAA. Thus, it's pure Spirit Energy that is used to create even those "lower" realms and dimensions. The only difference is that the physical universe is much more condensed than the VOID, aka the KHAA.

As we know, this universe is based on the Law of Freewill. With such a free form of creation, a lot of responsibility came as a result. So much could go wrong, but that was taken into consideration. After all, it was an experiment that was innovative and fresh, and if it worked out, it could be a fantastic way to expand not only the Orion Universe, but everything, including the Monad, understanding Himself better. However, from our human perspective, there is a downside to this, as well...

Good and Evil

We humans, because of what we learn in this construct, distinguish between "Good and "Evil," considering them opposites from each other. But instead of thinking in opposites, why not thinking in parallels? Good and Evil exist side by side; it's a choice, using freewill to make that choice. But as always, the person who makes the choice must be ready to take the consequences, good or bad. Or, hopefully, the person will learn something from either experience.

If good and evil are free choices, why choose good before evil? Because of the consequences. If the person has genuine empathy, and he or she projects evil onto others, that person can imagine how it can feel for his targets; how it is to be at the receiving end of the spectrum. Does the empathic instigator want that to happen to himself or herself? Probably not. Those who have made previous choices to gain something without having to do the work, manipulatively using others to get what they want, may become insensitive to empathizing with the receiving party over time. Evil within them may prevail because the consequences don't happen instantly in this reality (cause and effect). But in general, it's a matter of short- or long-term consequences. Most people want to avoid pain—physical or emotional—both in self and others. Existence becomes easier that way, and it's more likely that those who regularly make "good" choices will avoid getting themselves into meaningless and endless disputes. Making proactive choices rather than reactive choices results in a higher frequency, which also affects the environment. Meaningless quarrels, and worse, are a hindrance to creation, which would be the reason the Queen wants more empathetic and compassionate creator gods; it also speeds up creation and expansion. Regardless of choice, any consequence is still a part of creation in the sense that it contributes to the knowledge of the outcome of manifested potentials. Still, choosing "good" before "evil" is, for the most part, preferable if we want a greater expansion of the Universe. The reason this is more pro-expanding is because that's how energy works. Disputes, arguments, fights, and all the rest of it are just directed energies bumping into their counter-energies. They are forces, stuck in a fight with each other, each to gain more control and energy for themselves, usually by stealing energy from the other party, and therefore delaying real expansion.

Feminine vs. Masculine Revisited

I believe the Nag Hammadi texts are quite correct in the spiritual part of their philosophy, but there is one thing I disagree with. That is the presentation of the Monad as masculine. When we talk about masculine and feminine while discussing these metaphysical terms, we are not talking about men and women. These terms are often confused. We talk about the feminine aspect of Spirit as the original creative force, the inside force, and the masculine as the "outside" force, executing the feminine creativity. Both exist in the same individual. Therefore, as I see it, the Monad can't be masculine because creative thoughts, which must come first, are feminine; it always starts there. For instance, if you want to create a clay figure, the idea and the image first forms inside your mind (feminine), and then you create it by sculpturing it on a table (masculine). It's the same principle as the Monad. If anything, the Monad is feminine rather than masculine, just like Sophia, and later in the process, the Queen. She is feminine but uses her masculine side to create in the developing worlds, which to a large degree are created with technology. Hypothetically, one could say that the Monad, at its very essence, and the way we can fathom it, is neuter, until it becomes "conscious" and starts creating. Then, "It" becomes feminine, and later, masculine. But creation *always* starts with the feminine aspect.

7: The Overlords' Exit Promises

Contract Between Orion and the Overlords

No one knows what went on in En.ki's mind before and during the Titan War and the Second Construct. Was he treacherous already from the beginning? Did he "secretly" work together with the Khan Kings (Sirians) from the get-go, orchestrating the entire destruction of Tiamat? Or did his rebellious thoughts not come to mind until the end of the Atlantis Era?

Although some things are unclear, there are hints we can follow up on. After researching and connecting dots, some of it based on conversations with an Orion source (*the* Orion source from now on), it seems unlikely that En.ki planned the invasion of the solar system. It was a Sirian inside job, as already discussed—a potential confusion regarding the contract between the Sirian Empire and the Orion Empire. Therefore, it's reasonable to expect that En.ki did not fight on the Sirian side in that war. Whatever the case, he took advantage of the situation later.

To recap a little: After the destruction of Tiamat, and after an Orion court ruling that it must be further established who owns what, En.ki had free hands to continue the Experiment in the solar system, which he did in the physical realm, where he was a genetic expert and could use technology. He knew the technology very well regarding how to create species among the developing worlds. After discussions back and forth with the Orion Council, he got the green light to set up the Experiment on the new planet Earth. The question is, was he still loyal to Orion, or had his rebellion already formed inside his head? We know he got a narcissistic injury when he was demoted to being second in rank under his younger brother during the Tiamat Experiment. Therefore, we can safely presume he at least held grudges.

I could not find trustworthy information on how long the Second Construct lasted, but it appears that En.ki mostly behaved, although I'm sure he didn't like that Orion took control over *his* Experiment. He was the creator of the physical homo sapiens bodies after much hard work figuring out how to animate this species. Therefore, Tiamat was the Queen's

Experiment, but Earth was his. That's how he reasoned. He did apparently disregard that Orion never gave him permission to create a *new* experiment on Earth that could be called *En.ki's Experiment*—he was merely allowed to be the builder of the new world, where the Queen's offspring could continue the failed Tiamat Project.

It becomes shady when he and Isis gave birth to Horus, which was the first incarnation of Marduk's Avatar on Earth. Was that planned, or did Marduk hijack the body without En.ki's and Isis' consent? We don't know, but I find it unlikely that En.ki and Isis would give birth to Horus without knowing Marduk would take the body. If my suspicion is correct, it means that we now have a point in time when we can highly suspect En.ki had planned his revenge and possible takeover of Earth, if not even Orion, at that point. We know he wanted humankind for himself, and it had little to do with his love for us. Unless Marduk forced himself into that body, why would En.ki/Osiris agree to letting Isis give birth to Horus if he despised him for having destroyed his mother's experiment on Tiamat?

There is little doubt that at the end of Atlantis, when En.ki experimented with genetics left and right, he was planning on creating new and "better" bodies for us that would suit his first attempt to create a Singularity—bodies that suited *his* Agenda better in what he considered *his* experiment. It is well known among alternative historians that the end of Atlantis was a highly technological era. I also have grounds for my suspicion when I review the wealth of communication I have archived between me and the Orion source. There I found a reference, where it states that the main reason for Orion to instigate the Flood was En.ki mixing human DNA with his and others' extraterrestrial DNA. That is precisely what he also has done in *this* construct. Already in the beginning of the Matrix, En.ki and Isis, and later Marduk and Ereškigal, mixed their genes with that of humans. It is the same pattern. Then they could insert parts of themselves into our bodies through our ancestry DNA, so they can easier manipulate and control us. This is the same principle as when we say we are affected in present time by our own ancestral line. When En.ki and Isis created the first mixed bloodline in this construct, it was the first major step toward a Singularity. This happened thousands of years ago. Now, they only needed to take over our minds enough to have faith to manage putting us into a Singularity and get away with it.

When Prince Ninurta and Orion saw what En.ki had done at the end of the Atlantis period, they knew the Queen's Experiment was void. It was destroyed and could not be preserved. So, as a better alternative, it was decided to wipe out life on Earth and let the 3-UCs return to Orion.

When it dawned to En.ki he would never be in control of humankind so long as Orion was breathing in his neck, he lied to Orion and set up a new private experiment, free from Orion snooping, and without asking Orion for permission. The new experiment should be entirely his. However, he seemed to "forget" that the beings he was going to populate his experiment with were the Queen's beings (the 3-UCs). He created the Matrix with a Dome and a Grid to keep Orion out and humankind in, whereafter we have had a very hard time reconnecting with Orion and the Queen. At this time, I think En.ki's mind was fully occupied with creating a full-fledged Singularity with "his" human children as cannon fodder and Avatars to ride into Orion and take it over. In his introject, he did nothing wrong. Others did the wrongdoing. This was *his* experiment, and the 3-UCs were his property because he provided us with physical bodies and had created a new experiment as far as we humans were concerned; in his mind, we had become his babies, and Orion was treating him badly and unjustly. In his thoughts (if we follow common narcissistic thought patterns), he considered himself grossly undervalued, and he was going to show his mother, Khan En.lil, and his annoying brother who is the smartest, and who is best fit to run Orion. "And just look at your children, mother. Your human soul group is weak and can't even defend themselves against me and my people, although they are many times greater in number. You want them to run the Universe as creator gods? Look how easy it is to manipulate them!" he thought. And the Sirians, of course, agree to such a mindset because in their reality, the cruelest and the strongest deserve to rule.

But none of them understands the first thing about Spirit because they never possessed it. They think the most ferocious and forceful beings should be in control of the rest. It's not so at all; the Universe needs compassionate and empathetic beings as creators; but the Overlords don't understand compassion, and they don't even have compassion for themselves.

When En.ki had established himself in the Matrix, and we humans were procreating again, Orion found this new, hidden construct, and reached out to En.ki. After arguing back and forth, an agreement, a contract, was created. En.ki had locked himself and the human soul group inside the Grid, so Orion could not get in without destroying the Grid. This they didn't want to do because the Grid comprises the mass consciousness of the human soul group, and to demolish it would be counter-productive—particularly at that stage. We had amnesia, and the BLA was now set up. Our bodies were much denser than the Atlantis bodies, so we could no longer remember who we are. Thus, Orion could not get our consent, and the consequences of destroying the Grid were not pretty.

The following was included in the agreement between En.ki and Orion: En.ki could continue the Matrix experiment without Orion's oversight if he promised to let us evolve and then set us free. He promised to do so, but being a trickster and a master manipulator and persuader, he broke the agreement without technically breaking it. He created his own ascension program within the Matrix system, which at least *appeared* to lead out of the Matrix system long-term—*very* long-term.

More on En.ki's "Ascension Program"

It is highly unlikely that En.ki's ascension program leads out of the Matrix even long-term. What we learn about his program is that each "dimension" can take a million years to complete. According to the RA Material, the Fourth Dimension (the Fourth Density, as they call it) takes about a million years to complete. So, what is it supposed to achieve for us? What can we learn there that takes so long? Apparently, we will learn and practice compassion for a million years. Hmm... and that comes from the Overlords who don't understand compassion. Look who's talking.

Aside from that, far from all humans will climb "up" the ascension rungs. Many are manipulated into taking another route, becoming spirit guides. After holding this position for a long time, they may get "promoted" to becoming teachers, meaning they will be channels/mediums for humans here on Earth.

Since having followed a variety of channeled material over the years, I find it unlikely that anyone ascends at all within this closed system. Still, that is justified by the Overlords by taking some of us out of the reincarnation cycle and putting us on "loftier" tasks. Thus, they let us "evolve." I would argue that the humans who become spirit guides, and later teachers, will not ascend at all. Instead, they descend, in the sense they get even more indoctrinated by the Matrix System, becoming even more loyal to En.ki. So far, from what I've heard, no one has graduated from the Matrix (except maybe recently, since a few people who have followed my revelations about the Grid have died within the last few years and have hopefully left the Matrix). The Overlords most likely justify our lack of graduation by convincing themselves they gave us all the chances to exit, but we screwed it up. Instead of following the narrow path to freedom, we continue following others (the Overlords), rather than thinking for ourselves and doing inner work, which would give us insights on how to best exit. Having these kinds of justifications handy, the Overlords think they can get away with it in a hypothetical future cosmic court. They won't!

Another justification is even more entitled and delusional. They think they can justify the lack of graduation so far with the fact that they will create the Singularity. When that is in place, the Overlords can let us all free to exit the Matrix. Thus, En.ki and the Khan Kings have kept their end of the bargain. Oh, there is a caveat, of course: The Overlords will come with us, and they will be so eager to keep the bargain that they will ride our Avatar all the way to the Queen's Court.

8: The Overlords' Internal Affairs

The Abyss, Better Termed "The ABZU"

I asked the Orion source during my WPP years where En.ki currently dwells, and the answer was he is still in the ABZU (or ABSU). Earlier on, I said En.ki dwells in the Abyss, thinking it was the same thing as the ABZU, but reviewing my files, I found out it's not. The Abyss is usually another term for the VOID, as I now understand it. The ABZU is what the old Sumerian mythology calls "the carcass;" it's a term for the bottom of the deepest chasm of the Matrix—the lowest section of the astral, sometimes called the "Hell Dimension." This is discussed in the Vedas, Egyptian mythology, Nordic mythology, the Eddas, the Babylonian texts, the Nag Hammadi, and elsewhere. When his brother Ninurta castrated him, making him "impotent," En.ki was cast out of Orion (Heaven) and "chained" in the ABZU, figuratively speaking. He is, since then, trapped there, stripped of his creative abilities. Of course, this is what the Bible calls the Fall of Satan and the Angels of Heaven. Archangel Michael cast them all out, and they fell to Earth. And as the legend tells us, Satan lives in Hell, which is in the Underworld.

What does it mean to be stripped of one's creative abilities? We don't know for sure, but taking that term into context, En.ki was thrown down into the pit, where the density is extremely low, metaphysically speaking. This denotes he cannot move around freely; it's too dense, and he can't move up to the levels of the KHAA where he can use the energies in the KHAA or take a body. I would suggest he is in an "electronic prison;" and that he is trapped inside a specially designed "grid," created for him by Ninurta as a punishment for what he had done.

This doesn't mean he is completely impotent, however. Although his soul-mind is trapped in the ABZU, he can still shoot off fires into the upper realms, but he can't do anything else with them than to shapeshift and observe. And when he shapeshifts, he can only stay in that form for a short period, while the energy lasts. I would argue he rarely does this because it's too draining, and energy is sparse.

The Greys and the Dracos

The Khan Kings, or at least most of them, were also stripped of their creative abilities, but they were not chained in the ABZU like En.ki. The ABZU imprisonment was Ninurta's retaliation; a punishment for having raped Isis. Marduk would probably have gotten the same treatment if he wasn't lucky enough to be earthbound in a human body, where it was, and is hiding from Orion. It's harder to get to him from outside the Matrix. After all, En.ki was in Rigel when he was castrated and chained. Still, on a soul-mind level, they are apparently all stuck in the lower dimensions, which the Pleiadians call the Machine Kingdom. We humans are now about to join them there in the Singularity.

The Khans have an advantage before En.ki, however; they can take bodies in the lower sections of the astral, which is below us in frequency. But these are cyborgs, and most of them are what we call the Greys—bodies that are resilient to the harsh conditions in the physical realms and in the Cosmic Water. So, they need to use these Grey body types to enter our Earth frequency, radiated from Saturn. We have all heard about the Roswell Incident in 1947, and the coverup that followed. Still, much information has leaked since then about how they found dead bodies of typical Greys, and they dissected them, finding they were half biological and half machine (they were cyborgs). Two flying saucers the Khans used to browse the solar system with entered our atmosphere, but something went wrong, so they crashed. Or the military might simply have shot them down—we don't know. A third option is that these crafts might have manifested inside our atmosphere by mistake, and they crashed.

I have nothing to back up the following statement with, but it's quite logical, in my opinion: The beings people say they have encountered in the Secret Space Program (SSP), the so-called Dracos, are Khan Kings in "space suits," i.e., their resilient cyborg types of bodies. It was Corey Goode who said in an interview with David Wilcock that this huge Space Commander, the infamous White Draco, seemed to be artificial intelligence. If it is true Corey encountered this tall, intimidating being, it confirms my theory to some extent. But there is more. Why do we call them Dracos? Well, it's because people say they come from Alpha Draconis. Are they really? Are those inside the Draco "space suit" from Alpha Draconis, i.e., Thuban? Yes, many of them probably are.

In the WPP, I discussed it briefly. Alpha Draconis is not inhabited by Reptilians, but the star system was once invaded by Marduk's forces—probably before the War of the Titans. The inhabitants who survived became prisoners of war and slaves to Marduk and the Khan Kings. Thus, it makes sense that the so-called Dracos come from Alpha Draconis in a manner of speaking. However, they are still Sirian Khan Kings. Maybe this tall Commander in a Draco Reptilian suit was Marduk? Unless the entire Draco apparition is a coverup memory.

The Grey bodies, in conjunction with the Reptilian bodies, probably work great as cyborg "space suits." Inside those suits are the Khan Kings. If we think about it, we have reptiles on Earth, in form of animals. Such beasts can be quite resilient. Their bodies are like armor, and it's difficult to fight them. Mind you, space is not a vacuum, as we've been told, with a temperature of 2.7 degrees Kelvin, minus 455 degrees Fahrenheit, or minus 270 degrees Celsius. Space is cosmic water (Spirit), i.e., waveforms. So, the Overlords don't need these resilient bodies to fight low temperatures. They need them to function in the Cosmic Water and in battle.

Ayahuasca Experiences in the Machine Kingdom

I know of a few people who took Ayahuasca and involuntarily visited the Machine Kingdom, without having heard of it before. One such person is a female life coach who is not into "conspiracies" at all. She said on her YouTube channel it was a very artificial place, where everything was machine–even the "living" creatures were machines. It was an extremely dark place, spiritually, and it gave her panic attacks while visiting it. When she made the video, she still had panic attacks (PTSD) from the experience. She considered this to be Hell and said she never wants to take Ayahuasca again. This is the realm the Overlords want us to descend to, and so far, we are rapidly on our way there as a human soul group.

Is the Earth Descending or Ascending?

I think many of us, who are on a self-exploring path, are experiencing the same thing. This reality is decreasing in frequency, and it is because of the very intense manipulation right now on a global scale. I would argue it's the fastest frequency drop we have experienced since the creation of the Matrix. Many people who are healing and connecting with their spirit body complain about fatigue, headaches, and even depression. I think that is because we feel the depletion of energy in this Matrix system, but also because of the density drop. The chasm between those who are increasing their awareness and those who are descending widens rapidly, and we feel it. There is a constant tiredness that does not go away with plenty of sleep.

If NASA's uptake of the noise, i.e., the frequency emitted from Saturn is accurate, it sounds extremely eerie and is very low in pitch. This is the frequency that is transmitted to Earth.

Some readers may now ask themselves the following: If the Overlords want us to descend to their frequency band, why not just project the desired frequency from Saturn onto us right away? Problem solved.

It's not that simple, from my understanding. We have physical bodies that work within our unique frequency band. If they lower the frequency transmitted from Saturn too much and too fast, our bodies will probably self-destruct. They must be careful. Hence, they want us to become cyborgs, which will noticeably change our frequency. That, in itself, together with Metaverse, will lower our vibrations, and we will become more solid. At that point, they can probably more lower Schumann's Resonances significantly; even those controlled from Saturn.

Thoth hinted in "The Emerald Tablets of Thoth" (allegedly about 36,000-38,000 years old) that the Council of Nine dwells "below," in the Underworld. Also, think Nergal and Ereshkigal from the WPP; they dwell in the Underworld. Thoth said there is a tunnel leading from the Sphinx in Egypt directly to where some gods have their residence, and Marduk has his own chamber there (or at least he had 36-38,000 years ago). Curiously, there are archaeologists today suggesting there is a tunnel system below the Sphinx. But the Egyptian chief archaeologist, Zahi Hawass, refuses to let foreign archaeologists explore that area.

En.ki's and Marduk's Father-Son Issues Explained

As discussed earlier in this book, Marduk is not En.ki's cosmic son, only the *physical* son from being born as Horus. Since the lifetime of Horus, Marduk has allegedly incarnated here on Earth lifetime after lifetime, just like we humans do. The major difference, however, is that Marduk reincarnated over and over into En.ki's pure bloodline and did so up until the day he created his own bloodlines with Isis and Ereškigal. These days, I would suggest, he incarnates in the Marduk-Isis bloodline. Thus, he followed En.ki from the Second Construct into the Third.

Zecharia Sitchin, the late translator of the Sumerian tablets, wrote that the gods left the planet after an internal war between Marduk and Inanna (Isis) on one side, and many other gods, including En.ki, on the opposed side. This supposedly happened some 4000+ years ago, which is, timewise, approximately halfway through the Matrix construct[[34]]. Maybe this was the approximate timeframe in which En.ki was castrated and thrown into the ABZU. The rest of the gods, who includes Sirians, were also stripped of their creative abilities and descended to a lower region of the astral. Left on the planet were Marduk, Isis, and Ereškigal, all three in human bodies of pure bloodlines. They were not part of the Orion punishment that was implemented on the other gods because these three were in human bodies. The rest of the gods apparently possessed and took over already occupied human bodies and hosted them, while the original souls in those bodies were temporarily overpowered and no longer in control over the body. I would argue they used En.ki's pure bloodline to do so. More about that kind of possession later in this book. In New Age circles, this phenomenon is called a "walk-in[[35]]."

Marduk now became Satan, The Lord of this World, and this fit him like hand in glove. Although Isis fled from him, so he no longer could continue that bloodline, Ereškigal was happy to take over the task[[36]]. Marduk now probably felt he was the one controlling Earth. This was not entirely correct, however, because En.ki can still communicate with his team of loyal Elites here on Earth from his position in the lower realm. Still, Marduk was, and is, here at Ground Zero, able to manipulate things firsthand.

I am sure En.ki was quite unhappy with his situation and his limitations, and he didn't like that Marduk had free range on Earth. He and his "son" are not exactly close buddies. Still, they are both working on the same goal to leave the Matrix and taking out Orion, although their ideas of how it is going to be done differ in the details. Both want to be in charge. Marduk, of half Sirian bloodline, has a lot of the Sirian competitive genes, where only the strongest deserve to survive. His view on his "father" is quite ambivalent because he both needs him and wants to get rid of him. En.ki is the master geneticist, while Marduk is not a scientist at all. Therefore, Marduk must learn from his father's technological advancements here on Earth, manifested in all this "innovative" nanotechnology we see developing in jaw dropping speed right now. This is Orion technology, misused by En.ki, and transferred to us humans to implement to create the Singularity. The term for this is "Technological Transfer Program" (TTP)[[37]]. So, Marduk needs his own scientists to learn from the technology En.ki floods the Earth with. In juxtaposition, Marduk wants to get rid of En.ki because so long as En.ki is alive, he is a threat to Marduk's chance of being the King of Orion—the Emperor of the Universe. They both want that position, and there can only be one KHAN.US KHAN.UR (King of the KHAA, or the King of Kings). Therefore, En.ki must get rid of Marduk, as well, in one way or another. This is the father-son issue they have.

A Previous Race Between En.ki and Marduk

Barbara Marciniak's Pleiadians tell us we humans, in a previous Singularity, attacked En.ki's remote stronghold in the Pleiades as cyborgs. According to them, there are still many human cyborgs there, ruling at least one of these star systems with an iron fist. The Pleiadians, channeling through Marciniak, say they are renegades from that nightmare, and they want us to help them change the timeline, so the invasion never happened. The Pleiadians report to En.ki, who grades them in their interaction with us humans. They say he is a "tough teacher."

It is my current conclusion that the invasion of the Pleiades by us humans in a cyborg form was not happening because we figured out who En.ki is, while we were in a previous Metaverse. Instead, I believe we were manipulated by Marduk to invade because Marduk wanted to shatter En.ki's stronghold, and he used us to do it. If this is true, I would further suggest that the previous Singularity was led by Marduk, not by En.ki.

Moreover, it's plausible that we were not in Metaverse at all back then. Instead, we were in Grey, cyborg bodies, still in the Matrix. Through stargates and hubs, maybe in hollowed-out crafts, controlled by Marduk, we invaded the Pleiades.

9: Nation Against Nation—En.ki vs. Marduk

Two Camps in Conflict

Maybe one could say there are two main opinions among researchers about political world conflicts. I am talking about political tensions between nations, and whether it's all for the show. My take on this is that it's both about tension and it's for the show. Mainly, it's tension, and this tension is that between En.ki and Marduk.

It's the father-son issues again. En.ki and Marduk both want to be in control of humankind, and in common Sirian manner, Marduk fights to take the top position and eventually wants to get rid of his father. This is just common sense because it's Sirian mentality. Sirians don't share power. En.ki might not initially want the competition, but I think Marduk's temperament forces En.ki to defend and protect himself. This means he wants to get rid of Marduk, as well, or the two will need to fight things out in the KHAA. However, if their cosmic troops are not united, the chances are less they will be victors in a future cosmic war. Both En.ki and Marduk want the Singularity because it's the only way for the Overlords to get out of here, but they both want it on *their* terms. And we need to remember that Marduk is the KHAN.US KHAN.UR, the King of Kings, among Sirians. He can never afford to be "weak." If he shows any kind of vulnerability, other Sirians notice it, and they see an opportunity to overthrow him and take his place. They will kill Marduk, and a new KHAN.US KHAN.UR will succeed him.

En.ki has the advantage of being the scientist, able to use Orion technology in his favor, but he is also handicapped, being in the lowest of realms with no chance to get out without humanity's help. But first he needs to gain humanity's trust, i.e., he must continue making us think like him, until we vibrate similarly. Then he can merge with our minds and ride our Avatars. And for us to vibrate as similarly to him as possible, we must come to *him* because he can't come to us. Thus, the part of the Elites who support him does all they can to lower the frequency of the human soul group as we speak. Marduk is doing the same because he also needs the human soul group to vibrate lower.

Marduk has the advantage of being on site, and he can manipulate matters more freely on the Earth's surface, having personal encounters with his team. His handicap, however, is his lack of scientific knowledge, so he must trust his own elite scientists, who learn from studying En.ki's technology in the order it is released upon this world. This means Marduk is technologically usually one step behind. One of Marduk's innate strengths is his conquest skills. As a Sirian, this is his specialty. Therefore, he is exactly where he needs to be; he is on Earth, where things happen. Here, he can be the perfect strategist; he can instruct his generals face-to-face and give appropriate orders. En.ki does not have that privilege from the place he is at. He must delegate the tasks remotely through his human minions.

To us humans, it matters not who of these two gods is the victor. Either way, we lose, unless we can get out of here. A bleaker option would be that we humans get together as a soul group and say "no" to this insanity. After that, Orion can come, heeding our unified call for help. I see no signs that this is going to happen, though, and neither did the Orion source.

En.ki vs. Marduk Supporters Among Nations

If there are two factions of world nations, sometimes working together and sometimes fighting each other, how do we know who is who? Which nations work for En.ki, and which one's work for Marduk? Once we get an insight into this, it becomes easier to understand why certain nations invade each other, and why other nations are eager to overthrow dictators or monarchs, ruffling their feathers in territories where they don't belong. By understanding the following concept, we also understand there is a deeper agenda behind invasions, assassinations of political leaders, and other shocking events, leading to something else that benefits either side (and sometimes both sides) of the covert battle between the gods.

As usual, it is we regular humans, way down on the totem pole, who must do the dirty work. We are the ones they send to war under false premises, killing and dying for the criminal Overlords, regardless of which side we're fighting on. We are the cannon fodder. In the meantime, our leaders sit safely in their offices, usually making sure their sons and daughters don't need to go to war.

During the WPP years, I was discussing this matter with the Orion source. I was told the monarchies of the world work for En.ki. The late Queen Elizabeth II, for example, thought she was Orion's representative on Earth, when she was nothing of the sort. Remember, En.ki is also from Orion. The monarchs (the queens, and the kings) are of En.ki's pure bloodline, i.e., the Noah bloodline of Osiris (En.ki) and Isis. This is important to remember as we continue through this chapter. Therefore, we can see or trace nations supporting En.ki. Another good indicator is to notice in what countries nanotechnology is the most innovative. Those are usually En.ki nations. There is, however, a caveat to this: Nations invade each other, overthrow leaders, and take over. So, a nation that was once a monarchy under En.ki's banner can change ownership overnight and become Marduk's domain, turning into a dictatorship or some other kind of political structure, and vice versa. A typical example of this is Russia, which ones was ruled by a Tsar (En.ki's clan). Backed up by secret societies, which always work behind the scenes, Vladimir Lenin came around, and after him, the demonic Josef Stalin. The Soviet Union obviously made Tsar Russia into Marduk's domain. After that came Mikhail Gorbachev, then Boris Yeltsin, and eventually Vladimir Putin, "former" KGB. Although the Soviet Union is gone, it's still Marduk. The USA is En.ki. Thus, the constant tension between these nations.

How can the U.S. be En.ki? It's a republic (supposedly), and not a monarchy. Wrong. The U.S., as well as Canada and Australia, and others, are monarchies, run by the British Crown. It is not commonly acknowledged, of course, but besides that it is irrefutable, it is easy to see that the entire North America is under the influence of the British Crown. Canada even used to have letter stamps portraying the Queen of England. Contrary to what most people think, the USA has never been independent—it's an extension of old England. The War of Independence was just a farce; a game played by secret societies, particularly Freemasonry, to create a Second Atlantis, i.e., a technocratic society, leading toward the Singularity. Sir Francis Bacon, the Rosicrucian, Freemason, and En.ki supporter at the court of Queen Elizabeth I, wrote about this in detail already in the 1600s. But people still want to believe that the American Revolution and the Constitution are in our favor. History repeats itself. The USA has never been about people's freedom, although some Founding Fathers, not being Freemasons, might have been led to believe so. It was supposed to be and is an experiment in technology, so En.ki can continue where he left off at the end of the Atlantis Era, when he was interrupted by the Orion-instigated Deluge.

Dictators and Presidents run South America and are therefore Marduk's domains. Haiti, Mexico, and Brazil used to be monarchies but are now republics.

China has the technology, so it should be En.ki's domain, right? It's not. It's Marduk's clan. However, China was once a monarchy, but was taken over. The country is now being used as one of Marduk's technology centers as he and his scientists learn more and more about En.ki's Orion technology.

Japan is En.ki, and they are not in alliance with Russia. But what about World War II, Pearl Harbor, and the American attack on Japan? Should the USA and Japan not be on the same side? Yes, but neither En.ki, nor Marduk care about the life of people—we are just tools for them to achieve a goal. The Japanese American conflict in World War II was just convenient for future agendas. The U.S. government knew about the attack on Pearl Harbor before it happened but did nothing—very similar to 911.

Of course, the U.S. and Russia have almost always conflicted with each other, and there has been constant competition between the two; although sometimes, they also work together. The companionship between them is real, as well as the antagonism. As mentioned earlier, both En.ki and Marduk want the Singularity on their terms, respectively, but sometimes they need to come together on terms they both must agree with.

We also notice that in general, most western societies are En.ki's domain, and the eastern block is Marduk. Russia is in cahoots with China and North Korea, and they are expanding their alliance to include most countries in that part of the world.

Using these tools and this knowledge of who is who in politics, we can more easily trace the global intrigues, interests, and conflicts. We can also better understand why they happen, and who is who. Still, we need to keep in mind that nations are invaded, coups happen, and the opposite side takes over. Thus, we have revolutions, world wars, and other devastating events that change directions in world politics. Nations even attack themselves or allow an invasion of their country to change things around, such as with 911, which was obviously staged.

Another good example of En.ki's versus Marduk's team is Elon Musk versus Klaus Schwab of the World Economic Forum (WEF). Musk is presenting technology, telling us we can't stop the Singularity from happening, but we can make it better than what some people want it to be. Musk works for En.ki. He produces the implants, the Starlink, the satellites, and so on. And on that level, Marduk is coming along because he wants this, too. Schwab is the non-technological guy—he is the finance guy, just like the Rothschilds and the Rockefellers, Morgans, the Mellons, etc. They are all supporting Marduk.

Facebook and Zuckerberg are technology. They and Bill Gates are En.ki's people. The same thing goes for NATO, supported by En.ki nations, and not supported by Russia and the East. The Scandinavian countries are also En.ki. They are all monarchies, except Finland, which is a republic but has been under Swedish monarchical occupation in the past.

Africa, mostly, is Marduk, except perhaps for Lesotho and Swaziland, which are monarchies.

It is interesting to research the treaties between countries. We can easily see which nations are En.ki territory, and which nations are following Marduk's policies.

Adolf Hitler and the ARY.AN Race

Let's talk about WW II. Based on what we just uncovered, was Nazi Germany En.ki's or Marduk's project? It would be Marduk, with a charismatic dictator, Adolf Hitler, as the puppet leader.

How many who have read the WPP ever wondered why Hitler wanted to create an ARY.AN race? The ARY.AN race is the name of the entire humankind—all of us who belong to the original spirit group on Tiamat. So, what was Hitler after? Why did he choose the blond, "Scandinavian" race as a prototype for the future Superhuman? Well, it was not because Hitler was confused—he knew what he was doing. He was Marduk's puppet, and his task was to help his Master to create, or rather maintain, an archontic bloodline for the ARY.AN human soul group to incarnate into soon, after Germany had won the war. Purer bloodlines (purer from an archontic perspective) are always easier to control than those that are heavily mixed and diluted, which most bloodlines are these days. The Scandinavians are mainly of the Marduk-Ereškigal bloodline, and in the 1900s, the Scandinavian bloodlines had become quite archontic (for more information, see my book, "The Story of Isis and the War on Bloodlines).

The battle between father and son to get full control over the Singularity is all about bloodlines. This is very important to understand because this is why all these wars and conflicts never seem to make perfect sense. Yet they do! If we think in terms of bloodlines (the Seed Lines of the Gods), it makes perfect sense and fills in the gaps. So, bear with me for a while, and I will explain.

The excellent book, *The Spear of Destiny*, by Trevor Ravenscroft[[38]], tells the story of Hitler and his connection with the Superhuman race living underground (the Overlords—the actual power behind Hitler). He told the upper echelon of the Nazi Party he had met them, and he was afraid. They were terrifying. He was apparently shaking when he said it. It was these Overlords who told Hitler which race they wanted to breed. As we just discussed, the "Scandinavian race" is the Marduk-Ereškigal seed line. So, Marduk is popping up here again. Obviously, Marduk wanted his own seed line to be the seed line in the forefront. I would argue that he wanted to end the Enki-Isis bloodline in favor of his own, but to confuse the matter some more, Marduk wanting to keep the Marduk-Ereškigal seed line was a last resort—a matter of getting more in control of the human genome in preparation for the Singularity. So, the way our genome had developed over time, Marduk apparently thought it was a better option to create his own archontic bloodline together with Ereškigal instead of with Isis. This way, he also thought he could claim us through our much purer, archontic DNA.

This was planned for obvious reasons. First, it would make En.ki weaker because he could no longer manipulate his bloodline remotely if it was ended. Therefore, Marduk wanted (and still wants) to destroy the En.ki-Isis bloodline as much as possible. Second, Marduk wants his own bloodline, as pure as possible, to enter the Singularity, which means he, through DNA, can more easily manipulate this seed line because his own DNA is within them.

Hitler called Germany the Fatherland, and that Germans were superior to others. He also mocked the Mother Goddess by using an inverted swastika as the Nazi symbol. The swastika is originally a symbol for the Orion Queen. The Overlords spread the lie about Germans being a superior race, and Hitler knew it. From the Overlords' perspective, the Germans were just "useful idiots,[[39]]" prepared to go to the slaughterhouse, ending up like the executed Jews. Marduk's intention, according to the Orion source, was to sacrifice the entire German people to the gods. They were not the "chosen ones." This also makes sense, taking into consideration what happened during the war, and particularly at the end. Hitler sent Germans to war, where many died, but then he made the unfathomable "mistake" to invade Russia in the middle of the merciless Russian winter. There is a lot to say about Hitler, but he was not stupid. So, why did he invade Russia? He sent millions of troops to freeze to death on the Russian tundra. That was the beginning of the major sacrifice that Marduk, through his marionette, Adolf Hitler, had planned that would feed Marduk and his Sirian allies with immense quantities of soul energy. He failed in his plans, fortunately, because soon enough Berlin was attacked and occupied by the allies, and Hitler fled and ended his days in Argentina, of which there is enough evidence to presume this is true. There are indeed also postmortem pictures of Hitler, if genuine, where he appears to be in his 80s or 90s. It certainly looks like him. There are also Argentinians who have been interviewed, confirming Hitler lived there after the war.

Those who invaded Berlin were of course En.ki supporters (the allies), except Russia, which was Marduk's domain.

"Now, wait a minute!" you might say. "If that is the case, why were Germany and Russia enemies, and why did Russia help the allies to defeat Germany if they were both Marduk countries?"

Stalin was in on eliminating Germans because Marduk ordered him to. The Germans were supposed to be eliminated from the beginning, and Stalin was a part of making that happen. So was Hitler—the two worked together behind the scenes for the most part, and they were both working for Marduk. The reason why Marduk did not want the German bloodline for his future convenience is probably because the German seed line is that of Marduk-Ereškigal. Marduk wanted to keep the purer Marduk-Isis bloodline intact, which, in this case, is the Russian seed line (see Chapter 1 for more about the different seed lines). The Marduk-Ereškigal line was always a last resort. If we look at the former Soviet Union and today's Russia, there is very little mixing between races in Russia. "Russia is for Russians"—they are of the Marduk-Isis seed line. The purer the bloodline, the easier it is for Marduk to control it. We also must remember that the black Africans are the original En.ki-Isis seed line, starting with Ham after the Flood, and Hitler was big on terminating black people. More about the black people later in this chapter. However, not all Africans were black, and if we investigate the Monarchs of the world, we will probably find a mix of black people with some other races, or non-black people, whose ancestors migrated from northern Africa a long time ago—all of them with a significant amount of the En.ki-Isis seed line.

Hitler's task was not to win the war—it was apparently to destroy the En.ki-Isis bloodline together with the Marduk-Ereškigal bloodline, in favor of the Marduk-Isis bloodline. If Hitler had succeeded, Marduk would be on top of his game as the only one in control of a relatively pure bloodline. But he never got to complete his task. The allies intervened, and many Germans survived the war, as we know, although severely reduced in numbers.

Nazi Germany was obviously a step in the direction for Marduk to create his own Singularity, eventually excluding En.ki from the equation. The German people, and the German soldiers, were used as cannon fodder. The Germans were known to be very good soldiers, and the country was strategically positioned to fight against the allies.

Marduk had always had the disadvantage of not having access to Orion technology. However, by the time just before WW II, he had managed to "breed" a team of scientists that could help him precede En.ki's plans, such as Josef Mengele and Wernher von Braun. Or so he thought! He failed, and En.ki won the war. Many Nazi leaders were suicided, and others were executed, but the U.S. smuggled the best Nazi scientists to America in Operation Paperclip[[40]], and these brilliant minds were now working with En.ki. So, the war greatly improved En.ki's chances of winning the race toward the Singularity.

But even Hitler and his brilliant Nazi Elite were stupid in some ways because if Nazi Germany had won the war, they too would have been sacrificed together with the rest of the German people. This was something they apparently never took into consideration. Regardless of our position as humans, we are just tools for the Overlords to be discarded when we are no longer needed. We are the malignant narcissists' objects to them. It seems to me that En.ki is primarily a malignant narcissist with many anti-social (psychopathic) traits, and Marduk is a psychopath at heart (if he has one).

A Brief Introduction to Eugenics

Before we move on, it's imperative to understand that the history of eugenics and mass extinction of "unwanted genetics" did not start with Nazi Germany. Ironically, this movement took root long before WW II, in America and in England, the two main countries supposedly working *against* Hitler and his "Final Solution." Some instigators in the USA were Henry Ford (Ford Motors), the Rockefellers, and other Elite bankers and various Elite intellectuals[[41]].

Henry Ford was in the forefront of promoting eugenics to the American population. Long before anyone knew who Hitler was, he and his lobbyists had managed to convince about 65% of the American population that it would be beneficial for humankind if people with handicaps, or those mentally challenged, people with mental problems and disorders, and certain folk groups, should be sterilized. So, Indiana was the first state that implemented this with the blessings from the majority of the American population.

But it got even worse. People in mental asylums were deliberately given tuberculosis through their food, and they eventually died. This was too slow of a process, however, so they ended up just killing them on the spot to get it over with. Many people know that Canada was jumping on a similar bandwagon. In England, Winston Churchill was also part of this entire process and supported eugenics full-heartedly. As the reader can see, *it's all about bloodlines!*

Much later, Hitler and intellectuals, who later were to become members of the Nazi Party, connected with the American secret societies, hooked onto this, as well, and Hitler wrote to certain eugenicists in America, applauding their work. During the Nazi years, Hitler gave Henry Ford the Highest Order of the Nazi Party for his great work that inspired Hitler to initiate the Final Solution. Ford received the medal in person[[42]].

Thus, Marduk and En.ki have common goals, but they differ in some important details, such as in rulership. They both show very destructive and highly psychopathic traits, wanting a certain outcome that they both agree with, but they fight each other at the same time in a constant power struggle. If they were capable of working together in peace, they would much easier accomplish their goal, and we would already be in the Singularity. Instead, they destroy each other's bloodlines, so the other party has a harder time possessing their designated seed line, and therefore, it's going to be more difficult to control us humans. For us, this could be a blessing in disguise because if they continue diluting each other's bloodlines to an extent that they perhaps can no longer ride our Avatars. Wishful thinking, maybe, but isn't it hypothetically possible, though?

The Insane Migration of People Around the World

In the previous section, we talked about keeping bloodlines as pure as possible, so the gods can more easily attach to us humans when it is time to "ride our Avatars." Although the bloodlines are kept purer the higher up the hierarchies we go, the man on the street is a "hopeless" mix. More so these days than just let's say, 40 years ago. Since then, nations all over the world have opened their borders, both for war refugees, and lately, for anybody. This, of course, mixes up the bloodlines even more because people now crossbreed much more between the races. This is deliberate, of course, and as I see it, it's because if pure blood can't be found anymore (except among the Elite), it's better to mix everything, probably so that both En.ki and Marduk, respectively, can attach to more human bodies than if they stick to only the few who are purer than the rest. Their problem is that they need to be able to control about 3% of the world population, and even that seems to be a heavy task for them. All this because they fight internally. It's typical for psychopaths and narcissists, however, to act like this, which usually leads to their own failure. This is what we hope for.

It is interesting to go back to the migration from Europe to America in the 1700s. In the beginning, there were mostly white people, Chinese, and Germans, mixed with the English and other Europeans. America and Canada are En.ki's New Atlantis, so he wanted to occupy the North American continent. Through the Monarchies and occupied countries under his flag, he started with the Europeans and the Asians; the Chinese being hired as "slave labor." They were the ones who built most of the railways in the 1800s.

But En.ki's goal was not to bring the Marduk bloodlines to America, even though he was in control over some of them because of the countries he had occupied with the help from his loyal Elite. In fact, he wanted to mix his own African bloodline (the En.ki-Isis line) with the white and yellow races already living in the USA. Hence the slave trade, where they brought a lot of black people into the Americas. Over time, they interbred with the white people, and thus, he had his own Ham bloodline (En.ki-Isis) present in his Atlantis, so he better could control the population there and insert himself into them. Up to this day, there are African Americans in the U.S who are not heavily inbred with other races, which makes that bloodline quite pure; and behind the scenes, En.ki can manipulate the population in his New Atlantis.

To understand better who is in control of which people, we can't only rely on the genetics, although DNA is at the bottom of everything in this Matrix. En.ki's people are the black people, but it does not stop him from conquering the white race and others. Just like alien species might invade and occupy other worlds, the gods do the same thing here. This is how En.ki could get white people to settle in America because at that time, England, Germany, and I believe, China, were all En.ki territory, although there was no black population in these countries, and if there were, they were few. The white people are Marduk's people, which makes the American white people vulnerable to Marduk's manipulation. And as we can see, black and white people have disliked each other for a long time, to put it mildly. On a subconscious level, both races feel the other one is the enemy—En.ki against Marduk (white against black). But America is En.ki's answer to Marduk's intrusion in Europe with his bloodlines. En.ki wanted a genetic research center that *he* was in control of, which is the USA, but also Canada, which came later. Now, his influence over America is substantial, while Marduk's genetic research centers are China and Russia.

Amidst all this, there are the Native Americans, who have suffered tremendously. Many of them claim to be survivors from Atlantis, i.e., of En.ki bloodline. As we know, the white man wanted to murder all Indians, and eventually ended up putting them in reservations. Here again, we have the clash between En.ki's people (the Native Americans) and the white Marduk people. Still, I think En.ki sleeps well at night, knowing that it will play itself out in the end, and he will be on top of it as soon as things calm down. So long as people interbreed, he's happy. He's got his Atlantis.

We must understand that almost everything here in the Matrix is about genetics/DNA. There is so much to know about this that the subject could cover a thick book, and perhaps I'll write such a book one day, after having done much more research, who knows? Either way, I think it would be worthwhile; keeping in mind how important this is for the Overlords. If it's important for them, it's important for us. Just know that we should be happy not to be of pure bloodline, or we would be much more easily possessed.

Maria Oršić and the Vril Society vs. the Thule Society

The Vril Society is a very interesting part of modern history. It was led by a young, beautiful woman named Maria Oršić[[43]]. She was born on October 31, 1895, in Zagreb, Croatia,[[44]] to Tomislav Thomas Oršić (mother's name unknown)[[45]]. The term *Vril* denotes the cosmic life force, i.e., spirit energy. Maria was a ballet dancer, among many other things, until she started receiving channeled messages so profound she teamed up with other psychic women. These ladies took Nordic names within the society, relevant to the messages they received, no doubt from En.ki's team. Maria claimed the channel originated from the star system Aldebaran in the Pleiades, where En.ki has (or had) a stronghold.

The Vril team, comprising only women, were obviously aware that the feminine energy was required for the clearest channeling, and the female body can more easily make this clear connection, exactly like the Orion source also pointed out, unrelated to the Vril ladies. Maria also grew her hair to her ankles, understanding that hair works as an antenna, through which she could transmit and receive energy from the cosmos.

The Vril ladies started channeling in the 1920s, when Maria was in her late 20s or early 30s. The most profound messages she received included blueprints of something that resembled saucer-like vessels, later called the Haunebu II[[46]]. None of the Vril ladies were scientists or inventors. They had no clue how these machines worked, but they were soon to find out.

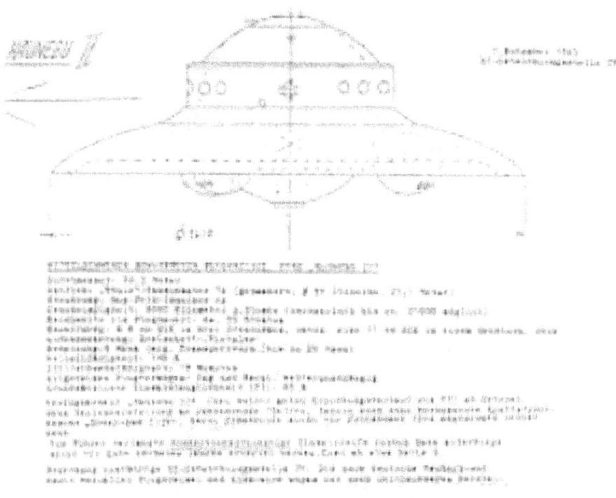

Fig. 9:1. Haunebu II blueprint[[47]]

In Germany, there was an organization called the Thule Society, or the Thule Gesellschaft—a secret society, founded in Munich shortly after WW I, in 1918, one year before the Vril society was founded by Maria Oršić. Thule was an occult society, based on Nordic mythology, but they chose the name after a mythological northern country in Greek mythology[[48]]. It was heavily sponsored by the Deutsche Arbeiterpartei (DAP), which later became the Nazi Party. Below is a quote from Wikipedia, which clearly states what these members believed in. These ideas later became the primary occult belief among the Nazi Elite.

> A primary focus of the Thule Society was a claim concerning the origins of the Aryan race. In 1917, people who wanted to join the

"Germanic Order", out of which the Thule Society developed in 1918, had to sign a special "blood declaration of faith" concerning their lineage:

The signer hereby swears to the best of his knowledge and belief that no Jewish or coloured blood flows in either his or in his wife's veins, and that among their ancestors are no members of the coloured races.[11]

"Thule" (Greek: Θούλη) was a land located by Greco-Roman geographers in the farthest north (often displayed as Iceland).[12] The Latin term "Ultima Thule" is also mentioned by Roman poet Virgil in his pastoral poems called the Georgics.[13] Thule originally was probably the name for Scandinavia, although Virgil simply uses it as a proverbial expression for the edge of the known world, and his mention should not be taken as a substantial reference to Scandinavia.[14] The Thule Society identified Ultima Thule as a lost ancient landmass in the extreme north, near Greenland or Iceland,[15] said by Nazi mystics to be the capital of ancient Hyperborea[[49]].

Here is another brief entry from the same Wikipedia article, and we will discuss this in more detail (my emphasis),

The Thule Society has become the center of many conspiracy theories concerning Nazi Germany, due to its occult background (like the Ahnenerbe section of the SS). *Such theories include the creation of vril-powered Nazi UFOs*[[50]].

I researched the Vril Society back in the days when I wrote the WPP, and I included some information about it there. However, there is always more to tell, and it is indeed a fascinating story. Clearly, the Thule Society was a Satanic society, based on Marduk's principles.

It seems to me that Maria and her team were serious about their channeling, and they were not Nazis—they unknowingly worked for En.ki.

They were his tools to bring technology into the world; probably to be presented to England or the United States.

But the Thule Society got informed about these fascinating ladies. They found out the Vril Society had blueprints of a new vehicle that ran on free energy—the universal Vril Power. Therefore, they infiltrated the society and took it over. History is vague about what really happened next, but I believe most researchers agree the Nazis forced the Vril ladies to work for them and to reveal everything they had channeled and learned. Thus, the Nazis had the technology to build flying saucers, called Foo-Fighters by the allies. After the war, the information on how to build these crafts went into American hands, and after that, people started seeing strange air vessels in the shape of flying saucers, capable or making odd movements and 90 degrees sharp turns. They were reverse engineered alien crafts, and the technology, obviously, was not supposed to come into the hand of the Nazis but the allies. And after WW II, the allies got hold of the technology.

What Happened to the Vril Ladies After the War?

There are many rumors about what happened to Maria and the others. Maria would have been 50 years old when WW II ended. Some suggest they were killed, while others say they fled in submarines together with a crew of top-ranking Nazis and selected German soldiers to live out their lives in South America.

But there is another rumor that refuses to go away, suggesting Maria, and perhaps the other Vril ladies, went to Aldebaran in the Pleiades and never returned. How would they do that, practically, if this is true? Well, the only way I can think of is that they were killed or committed suicide, intending to go to the Pleiades in spirit (as 3-UCs). Perhaps En.ki let them? There are no satisfying answers to what happened to this small group.

Technology Transfer Program and Military Betrayal

It is interesting to note that only a few years after WW II, in 1954, President Dwight Eisenhower met with two ETs at an air force base in California[[51]].

They were supposedly the "Nordics" (representatives for the Overlords). Eisenhower's granddaughter, Laura Eisenhower, has confirmed this encounter, and spoken of it in public.

But what did these Nordics want?

Obviously of the En.ki clan, they wanted to introduce a "Technology Transfer Program" (TTP)—an exchange program between the Nordics and the U.S. Government. In addition, they offered to share "spiritual knowledge" if the U.S. eliminated their nuclear weapons. Eisenhower declined because he wanted to keep the nukes.

The story goes Eisenhower also met with another ET groups, and this second group were the Greys, this time most likely sent by Marduk, trying to get humans to consent to alien abductions of both humans and cattle, so they could perform DNA tests on both. This seems like an attempt by Marduk to forego or catch up with En.ki's genetic science. The Greys promised to return the bodies safely afterward. It is unclear whether Eisenhower agreed, but it's my impression he didn't.

Instead, it later came to Eisenhower's knowledge that his own Military Industrial Complex (MIC) went behind his back and made the deal with the Greys. Since then, the Greys and the Government have mutilated cattle and abducted humans, apparently conducted horrific experiments on both. Cattles have been returned per the agreement, but eerily mutilated, done with unknown technology. Some humans are missing, but most were returned with their memories wiped out and cover stories implanted. Only during hypnosis have these innocent victims been able to recall what happened. The emotional trauma they go through during hypnosis is reportedly horrific.

In his farewell speech to the nation in 1961, President Eisenhower warned the American people in a public speech against the Military Industrial Complex, stating they were taking over America and are a massive threat to the Nation.

I suggest because of this treaty between the "Greys" and the MIC, the Secret Space Program (SSP), where they transfer humans into space to become "Super Soldiers," is just an extension of what happened during WW II. And reportedly, the SSP is run by Germans up to this day—some of them working off-planet. More about the SSP in a later chapter.

After World War II, since Marduk had lost his power, at least temporarily, he needed new consent from his enemies (the United States). He got that consent in a clever way by contacting the MIC, getting permission to infiltrate En.ki's technological program—even the Space Program. He could then, because of the American MIC's treacherous act, hijack people in their sleep and either do experiments on them or send them into space in a soul-mind state. So, he transferred their astral bodies (artificial soul) into cloned bodies of themselves that are apparently more resilient and can better withstand the "harsh conditions in space." There are many testimonies by Super Soldiers that spill the beans across the Internet. Most of them appear credible. There is no doubt the SSP exists; the only question is, what is true and what is not? We know both the military and the Overlords can induce false memories (cover memories) into the victims. Most Super Soldiers also admit they have been viciously mind controlled. Still, I believe there is truth to their stories.

The Previous "Singularity" From Pleiadian Perspective

According to Barbara Marciniak's Pleiadians, there was a previous "Singularity," in which we humans invaded the Pleiades and have created terror there up to this day. The reason the Pleiadians are here, from what they say, is because they want us to change the timelines, so the invasion of the Pleiades never happened. However, I have encountered no information from the Pleiadians where they tell us *when* this first Singularity took place. So, we can only hypothesize for now, and the following is subject to change but the hypothesis seems quite likely if we think in the context of what we already have concluded overall.

We have enough evidence from multiple sources and ancient texts that En.ki started messing with genetics by the end of the Atlantis Era in the Second Construct. Very few details have survived about exactly how far En.ki got before the Flood interrupted him. According to the Pleiadians, the technology that was used at the end of Atlantis was impressive and more developed than the technology we have now. They also mention that we had a well-developed space program (then there was no Grid or Dome at that time). My question is: did En.ki get so far as to create the first Singularity and implement it to a certain degree, promising some humans they would be as gods? If so, they only had time to introduce a fraction of humankind to that program.

Assuming this happened, did Marduk at some point hijack the first Singularity, turning humans against En.ki, their "creator?" Did Marduk manipulate us into attacking the Pleiades, En.ki's stronghold, attempting to "disarm" En.ki? It would certainly be in line with Marduk's behavioral pattern.

Could it be that this is when the Orions here on the planet discovered what En.ki and Marduk were up to and ended the Experiment before it was too late, and it would draw all humans into a new Construct, meant to be the "First Singularity?"

This would explain why only a certain number of humans fell for the manipulation and got stuck: the Flood interrupted En.ki's new experiment. Then, after the Flood, he and Marduk both entered the Third Construct—the Matrix—and then the race toward the Singularity started all over, but this time without Orion interference.

10: The True vs. Artificial 3-UC

A Deep-Dive into the 3-UC

In The Orion Book (Volume 1), I coined the term, "3-UC," which stands for "3 Unit Composite," i.e., soul, mind, and spirit body. Being a unique 3-UC means we are human because we are the only beings in the Universe structured in this way. Simply put, we are immortal because our true bodies (which I sometimes call the Namlu'u bodies) are our Spirit. In addition, we have soul and mind, like all other developing species in the Greater Universe, but we are "fused" into one unit made up of three components.

So, before we move on, let us recap a little.

Our spirit body is, per definition, made of spirit energy, or spirit fire (from Sophia's Spirit). Our spirit body comprises trillions of fires, which is defined as bioelectricity, assembled into a formed and shaped body, the so-called Namlu'u body. The Queen did this. The spirit fires are forming our Avatar, which is our true spirit body, and it has a certain shape; it is, in the KHAA, viewed as tall and slender, with black skin, and usually with red hair. It is purely ethereal (spiritual). There is nothing physical about it, like in "physical universe." This Avatar also makes it possible for us, the Namlú'u, to travel the Universe, bringing the spirit body with us. The Queen made our Avatars to operate in the KHAA immediately, while avatars that are planet-bound and star-bound lack this body. They are mind, soul, and *physical* body, and in its essential form, their soul is shaped like an orb. In their cases, soul and mind make up one unit (a 2-UC), and the physical body is separate and eventually deteriorates, just like our sapiens body. When the beings in the developing worlds choose to explore the KHAA and its spiritual dimensions, they must first abandon their body in the physical realm forever, and they now become a 2-UC (soul and mind, making up their Avatar). We were born in the spirit realm as 3-UCs, and our bodies were never physical—in fact, they are immortal Spirit. Therefore, on Tiamat, we had potential access to the entire KHAA from the get-go. We were planet-bound in the sense that our 3-UCs were to develop there from "infancy," but we could easily shoot off spirit fires into the KHAA to explore the KHAA at the same time as we stayed stationary on Tiamat, once we learned how to do it. Although we never got the chance to get to the point of graduation and leave Tiamat the way it was intended, the purpose was that once we graduated from the Tiamat Experiment, we could do what the 2-UCs on the developing worlds did; we could leave Tiamat. The difference is that once we leave our home world, we take our bodies with us, while the 2-UCs leave their physical bodies behind. To be human, we must fulfill the criteria of having soul, mind, and spirit body. If one of these components is missing, we are not human.

The way the Queen created us, we can travel the Universe, not only as a 2-UC but as a 3-UC. We can therefore think ourselves to any planet or star in the galaxy, land on or in it, and still keep the shape of Namlú'u bodies. As we have learned, the soul is defined as the vehicle or vessel that keeps the fires together, forming an Avatar, so beings can move around in the KHAA. The spirit body is our human Avatar. Our spirit body is constructed as such that it's forming a natural Avatar. We humans can shapeshift, just like the 2-UCs, but we shapeshift with our spirit body. When we then go back to our original shape, we form the Namlú'u body, while the 2-UCs go back to the shape of an orb. However, it should be mentioned regarding the 2-UCs out in the KHAA that it is common that these beings form an Avatar that is very similar to the physical body they once possessed because that's what they are familiar with.

When we, the 3-UC, leave our original world (and in the current case, the Earth), we already possess Spirit and can therefore immediately start working as creator gods in the KHAA on a level we can manage until we learn more. And we will theoretically have access to all dimensions in Orion. I wrote "theoretically" because after having spent thousands of years in this destructive construct, we might need to be somewhat rehabilitated before we go out there and let loose our creativity. At least, this is my presumption.

The 2-UCs, as discussed elsewhere, leave their developing world without a body, and they can enjoy what others already created in the KHAA, e.g., the spiritual worlds, in contrast to the denser and more restricted physical worlds. The spiritual worlds were, of course, created by the Queen, in conjunction with evolved 2-UCs, who eventually earned Spirit and started creating.

Many of the 2-UCs who recently have left the physical realm will eventually evolve in the KHAA and improve themselves to where they can get access to the higher KHAA dimensions, where they can use Spirit around them to create. But they never gain a spirit body. Therefore, they are not immortal, but still live as long as the Orion Universe exists, or someone destroys them with a terminator weapon (which is very rare). We humans would, in Spirit, survive the destruction of the Universe.

That is how the Orion Universe is set up to function. Broadly speaking, it comprises a physical realm of dense energy, which forms matter, and then there is another part that is pure spirit energy, in which advanced beings, called creator gods, can create what they prefer.

A Deep-Dive into the Artificial 3-UC

As usual, En.ki has mimicked virtually everything the Queen created in the KHAA and implemented it in the Matrix. However, the Queen is of Spirit, and En.ki is not. Therefore, En.ki can't create a universe such as Orion because he lacks the main component—Spirit. Thus, he must use technology to mimic the true magnificence of the Spirit Realm.

Not only does he mimic. He also inverts what the Queen created so he can keep us trapped here. By inverting the original creation, he makes us believe that what is true is a lie, and what is a lie is true. If someone makes a being believe the lies, that will, of course, keep that person trapped in the lies. Hence, we must detach from *everything* in the Matrix because everything here is a mirror of what is in the KHAA. Please ponder that...

Now, let us dive into the artificial soul and the artificial spirit.

The *artificial soul* and *artificial spirit* are frequently discussed in the Nag Hammadi Gnostic texts, but no one knows what these terms mean because no one who does not have the information about the true 3-UC can understand what the Gnostic scribes wrote down, based on the gods' dictations (En.ki and Marduk, and sometimes Thoth, i.e., the ludicrous Hermetic Gnostic texts). So, let's dig into it.

Now we know that our true selves comprise soul, mind, and body, where the body is of spirit. Even in the Matrix, we are composed of three fake parts: soul, mind, and "spirit" body. Let's see what En.ki did to create this illusion.

We, the true 3-UCs, are investing our Spirit energy in the Matrix, completely merged into this holographic simulation called 3-D; just like a player is engrossed in a computer game (a metaphor I've used a "million" times, but it works brilliantly). In the beginning of the Matrix, when we had become engaged in En.ki's Matrix game, mostly because of sex and other pleasures and excitements, he closed the trap, and since then, we the 3-UCs are investing our energy in this simulation, mostly unaware we are doing so. We, who have learned who we are, are also aware that our real 3-UC is locked into this System, but we know how to break free. Still, most 3-UCs don't.

So, En.ki, the mimicker, created a false soul, i.e., a false avatar that we must use in the Matrix, and that soul/avatar is the astral body, which also is a blueprint for the physical body. Therefore, our physical body is shaped in accordance with our false soul/avatar—they are mirrors of each other. One is metaphysical and the other is physical. This is why you look the way you look. En.ki is creating the souls/avatars and form them in the astral into astral bodies. The astral body is a "container," as it were, which the locked-in part of ourselves fill with spirit fire before each lifetime.

Again, we can compare this with playing a computer game. When you play, you get an avatar within the game that you will possess and control. Then, while playing, your avatar might die, and you need to possess a new avatar and start over from scratch. This is basically how reincarnation works.

So, you die on Earth and go into the astral in your astral body (the artificial soul), which is shaped exactly like your physical body, containing your spirit fires (and other's fire, too, as we shall see). While you are living in the Matrix, these spirit fires mainly contain the memories of your *most recent* lifetime because these are the fires that were operating inside the cells of your sapiens body, recording what was happening in *that* life.

Usually, the artificial soul that the true 3-UC inhabits, goes through the tunnel in the astral and into the light, and the memory of the recent lifetime slowly fades, and there is a reason for this. The astral workers want you to be somewhat amnesiac when you enter the recycling center, where you first go through a "life review," which is a very vicious process. Your recent life, which you by now only partly remember, is replayed for you. Although your good deeds will be acknowledged, the bad things you've done, or the not-so-good choices you made, will be emphasized. The astral workers then suggest you go back to Earth and take care of those issues in a new lifetime to straighten yourself out. This they call karma. Ironically, most of this "karma" is not even yours. Some of it is, other things the astral workers make up, and yet other things are the Overlords' karma. Well, isn't that handy for them? The Overlords commit crimes, and we make up for them, thinking they are our crimes. Therefore, the Overlords can swear themselves free because we take on their wrongdoings, creating the exact trauma bond they want us to create; one between us and the Overlords. Just like narcissists here on Earth, they create a shared fantasy and a trauma bond that glues the abuser and the victim together. When such an energy bond exists, the Overlords can more easily manipulate us both directly (like narcissists do) and by proxy, which is through the Elite bloodlines, and below them, the politicians, the media, the educational system, and all the rest of it. This is partly how they do it. They are preparing to ride our Avatar to Orion by merging with our minds and thus taking over our spirit bodies. Once they are in complete control over our minds, they are by definition also in control of our spirit bodies.

It should be noted here that karma is usually nonsense. I was told by the Orion source that karma is only valid if we humans believe it's valid. If we disregard the karma projected onto us in the afterlife, it won't affect us and is considered void. One could say that this karma is the soul contract between the Overlord and us—the soul contract so many truth-seekers try to break. It's easy to break. You just choose to break these "contracts" all at once because they were never valid. They were forced upon us, using lies, and narcissistic manipulation, projection, and gaslighting. I disregard all so-called karma, and I advise others to do this, too, although it of course is up to the individual.

But doesn't karma exist, though? If someone commits a crime, doesn't he or she eventually get caught and has to pay for it, whether through jail time or worse, depending on the crime? As the Orion source said, if this were true, the Overlords would have been caught and put to justice a long time ago.

The disincarnate, now feeling shameful and guilty over what they might or might not have done in the previous life, agrees to go back to Earth in yet another incarnation. Then the astral workers destroy the avatar, the artificial soul, and gather the spirit fires within it, mix them with other people's spirit fire in a big soup, and place this mix in a new avatar, who remembers nothing from previous existences. This will eventually create conflicts in the incarnated person's next lifetime. The avatar, i.e., the astral body, now has a new blueprint that looks different from the last incarnation, and then they shoot this avatar into a baby body within the same seed line in which they existed before. The spirit fires within the avatar are now mixed with others, but the 3-UC, controlling the avatar from "outside" the Matrix, i.e., still make up the genuine YOU. You are the player whose energy is contained within the Matrix avatar.

Then you "wake up" in a new sapiens body, shaped after the new astral blueprint, and you're confused and scared. You remember nothing, and your new personality is formed by what you learn from your parents, your environment, your ancestral DNA, and to various degree (mostly to a tiny degree) what your genuine 3-UC might bring to the table in the sense of "soul development."

So, where and what is the artificial spirit body in all this? You might have guessed it. *It's the sapiens body, of course.* Thus, the expression, "The body is your temple." This is also why many people "worship" their body or other people's bodies, are vain about them, and afraid of death. The spirit body is not supposed to die, but in this Matrix, our bodies die (what a mockery). Those with the least spiritual development, who don't believe in an afterlife, think they will die forever when their sapiens body dies because somewhere deep inside, they "know" the body is what should make us eternal. If the physical body dies, many people think they cease to exist. This is where fear of death comes from, which the WingMakers call the "death implant[[52]]."

So, in summary:

a. A genuine 3-UC comprises a true soul, mind, and spirit body in one unit. This being is immortal.
b. An artificial 3-UC comprises an artificial soul, mind (the astral body), and an artificial spirit body (the sapiens body) in one unit, but the entire artificial 3-UC is mortal and can only function within the Matrix.

In between lives, we were a fresh slate, a new beginning; something that had never really been done before this matrix. A being that had the opportunity to express itself in a way that would not hurt others, with 100% freewill involved, no proxy. That was the Orion-Khan agreement for this construct. The Khans stated we could never achieve this, and given the chance, we would mess it up. So they bet against Orion on this one. And from what beings outside the Matrix are noticing, they are proving their point. We have messed it up, but we most likely wouldn't if the Khan Kings were not involved, which they are, to a massive degree. Thus, where did the "no proxy" part of the agreement go? They have controlled us for thousands of years through our emotions. The Queen gave us this wide range of emotions that served us on Tiamat so we could complete our task. We were supposed to experience our emotions and be able to control them. Here in the Matrix, the emotions usually control *us*, at least until we have done our inner healing. The Invaders have used both our gifts of emotions and freewill against us.

For some narcissistic reason, the Khan Kings think they proved their point when we "messed up." So, I'll direct the following to Marduk and En.ki: Let's get this straight and help me understand here. You give us a fake life review from a life we barely remember because our memories fade in the astral. Apparently, afraid that we would actually make it, regardless of the traps and obstacles you set up for us, you need to implant karma that is yours into the being with a blank slate (memory wipe) and send him or her back with amnesia, to a so-called "freewill" life on Earth. Sure enough, we "mess up." Is anybody surprised? And where is freewill here on Earth? I don't see it. Isn't there something wrong with this picture?

And here is something else that is completely screwed up:

The 'payment plan' to pay off the debt that the Khans agreed with together with the Orion Council was that if we humans can evolve here on Earth by using our energies wisely and positively, and for the good of all, the Khans let us go, no strings attached. But if we don't evolve, they recycle us over and over until we do. However, when we start agreeing with the Khans, wittingly and unwittingly, we become "theirs" because now we no longer want to evolve, but instead follow the Khans' directives. Thus, Orion has no claim on us, but the Khans do. This is Khan logic.

But the Mother is tired of this and wants the "loan" paid off in full, i.e., let *everybody* free. But the Khans can't comply to this because they would obviously lose humanity, and also, the "pay in full" request came "too fast," and the Khans don't have enough forces to fight the Mother's forces. They also don't have enough energy to use in such a project. So now the Khans are referring to the Law of Freewill, and they tell Orion that the human soul group agreed with them. We were never forced to agree with them, the Khans say, but we did it out of "freewill," or so they claim. Therefore, in the Khans' minds, it's not their fault, but ours, and therefore we will be the ones, per definition, who must "pay off the debt." It's true that most humans want to stay here, though it's of course out of ignorance. So, Orion would break the Law of Freewill, from the Khans' perspective, if Orion invades and forces us to leave the Matrix. This is complete nonsense, but fact remains we need to wake up as a group before Orion can intervene.

En.ki, Marduk, and the Khan Kings abused freewill and used it against us, and therefore, they broke the contract. When a contract is broken, it is void, and the debt must be paid in full. This is exactly what Orion now forces upon the Overlords. The Khans are desperate because they don't know what Orion will do, and neither do we humans. But the fact is they have yet to set us free, and from what we notice, taking Metaverse and the Singularity into consideration, have no intention to set us free. They continue like before, but at greater speed. They sense they have little time to complete their tasks, something we are also experiencing; everything is speeding up!

Carl-Gustav Jung's Archetypes

Carl Gustav Jung was a brilliant man. Not only did he deeply explore our psyche, but he was also a great philosopher. He was the one who sorted the human mind into different archetypes, something that since then has been commonly used in character development by fiction writers. The entire "Hero's Journey" novel trope is based on the principles of archetypes.

In addition, Jung also explored something he called the shadow side, the subconscious mind, and discussed how to do shadow work.

I am certainly not an expert on Jung's archetypes, but I think I understand the concept to some degree. Archetypes can be good or evil (using human terms), and every person has all of them inside, from being angelic to the worst person perceivable. But we choose who we are, which archetype we want to focus on, and that becomes our primary personality. When the dark side inside us knocks on the door, we can choose not to open, and instead open another door, where a more benevolent archetype resides that better serves us positively.

We are what we focus on, and what we focus on is our choice, even when it's difficult to choose. So, if we possess a trait we don't like, we can hold back and change it to something we like. This is exactly what my 21-Day Program is all about[[53]].

Be kind to others, respect them, and don't be abusive or derogatory.

Many people feel sorry for their abusers or their narcissists. But the abusers know what's right and wrong, regardless of how innocent they say they are. They are fast to point out flaws and wrongdoings in others and judge them for it, while they themselves are doing the same things and worse, but covertly. They know right from wrong, but they choose to do evil. If they would genuinely choose a more benevolent archetype, and focus on it, they could, over time, become better people and, therefore, more loved. But they rigidly stick to a destructive archetype, and it's always by choice. We are our choices. Made a bad choice? Well, just make a better one next time.

The same applies to the Overlords. Fortunately, Orion knows this. The Overlords have chosen to stick to a very destructive archetype.

According to psychology professor Sam Vaknin, Jung is no longer taught in psychology classes. Is it because if people knew too much about archetypes, the Elite would have a harder time implementing a narcissistic society? It certainly makes you wonder, doesn't it?

11. More on the Between Lives Area

Why we Don't Need to Fear the Tunnel of Light

One of the most common concerns I hear regarding exiting through the Grid is people's fear that the pull from the tunnel of light will be so strong it will inevitably draw the discarnate human in. After that, the astral workers would recycle them once again, against their will.

To that, I have bad news, and I have good news.

I just learned from old notes, scribbled down during the WPP sessions, that the Overlords, of course, control the BLA, and an unsuspecting artificial soul that has just left the physical body will, if the astral workers see it appropriate, elevate toward the tunnel. They might feel a powerful electromagnetic pull toward it, and they just go with the flow. And indeed, they have little say in the matter.

However, those who disagree with going through the tunnel will *not* be drawn to it, whether or not they see it in the afterlife. The reasons the astral workers can pull people in are twofold:

a. we humans as a group allow them to. We have, in the Khans Kings' twisted logic, agreed to this treatment because we have agreed to be recycled over and over to eliminate our "karma."

b. the individual who is drawn into the tunnel, giving no immediate consent, will still be pulled in because in their lifetime here on Earth, they never, in their mind, disagreed about being recycled and going into the tunnel. This applies regardless of whether the person is aware of a tunnel of light.

Opposed to that, there are also two main reasons some people don't see the tunnel at all after death (we hear about this sometimes from people who have had Near-Death Experiences [NDEs]).

a. during their lifetime, they have studied this phenomenon and found it repulsive, saying to themselves they do not want to go that route because it seems "suspicious" to see Jesus, God, or Buddha at the end of the tunnel. They disagree with this route, even though they might not be aware of any other route. In these cases, it seems like these souls go to a waiting area, as discussed in Michael Newton's books on regression therapy addressing the afterlife[[54]]. These souls go before a council, where it is decided what to do next. Most of the time, the soul is eventually tricked into reincarnating again.

    b. The person, while still incarnated on Earth, chooses to leave the construct through a hole in the Grid. This means, literally, that the person now completely disagrees with the afterlife agendas. In those cases, the astral workers can do nothing except let these people go because they have already made up their minds. The astral workers must respect the Law of Freewill, particularly when they can't manipulate us anymore, and therefore, they cannot keep us.

This means that we, if completely determined to leave through the Grid, cannot be tricked into the light. If we see the tunnel, there will be no pull. We are free to go. The Orion source conveyed this to me. He said the Overlords are in control of the recycling process, but only because we let them. All we need to do is to disagree, and they cannot force us to take that route. It's all about consent—always (and the manipulation thereof). The reason En.ki is such a trickster god is because he tries to work his way around the Law of Freewill by tricking the target into giving consent, whether the consent is direct or indirect. If we see through that, there is nothing he or anyone else can do, and nothing to fear.

Keeping this in mind, you may even better understand why it's so important to disagree with everything the "authorities" try to force us to consent to. The mask fiasco is one example, the lockdown is another, and the WOKE culture is a third. Disagree with it all and don't give your personal consent to anything that goes against your morals and your ethics code.

In the previous chapter, we discussed the artificial soul and spirit and how the astral body is being destroyed by the astral workers. I understand this concept is scary to many readers, but be aware that it's not the genuine 3-UC that is destroyed; it's the energy that is invested in a certain artificial avatar is being demolished. Nonetheless, it creates amnesia in the 3-UC regarding the lifetime of that specific avatar, so long as the 3-UC is investing her energy in the Matrix simulation.

The brilliant Rudolf Steiner, who had seen through much of this over a hundred years ago, once said, and I paraphrase, "Only the spirit core survives the process of reincarnation, and only what in your lifetime entered into the deepest core of your awareness therefore survives." I have never seen it explained better. What he means is that even though they treat us as badly as they do here in the Matrix, and they give us amnesia on steroids, there is always this "core being," which is the genuine 3-UC—the spiritual us—who survives. And one day, after we have exited the Matrix, we will remember what was done to us because it is registered in our genuine 3-UC.

Choosing the Alternative Route

As we can see, we are heavily manipulated, both while incarnated and in between lives. They throw us hither and thither like marionettes, without very much say in the matter. We are indeed collateral to the Overlords and all their minions, and they treat us like objects they can mess with as they wish while accomplishing their goals. We are tools for them to help them get what they want. This mindset is, of course, psychopathic rather than just narcissistic. They have no respect for life, save their own—sometimes not even that.

We have discussed the astral body extensively in this book because it's highly important to understand what it truly is and how it works on us. But ancient texts, present time psychics, and various researchers talk about more than one light body. The most common number mentioned is that we possess seven of them, each one having a certain purpose. For example, one is the emotional body, which encapsulates our emotions, while still in the Matrix, and I would suppose that when we die, this body is destroyed as well, so the Overlords can accumulate that for themselves and use it as food, and for other purposes (such as stabilizing the energy of their stargates and portals). Another body supposedly stores the memories from our most recent lifetime, and this is presumably the body that slowly deteriorates after spending some time in the astral after death. There are more light bodies, but there is no reason to go into all of them because they become irrelevant after we have exited.

None of these bodies will survive the exit. You leave the Matrix in your artificial body, but as soon as you enter the KHAA outside, you merge with your real Avatar—your 3-UC, or more accurately, your spirit body. In other words, you withdraw your energy (your current human personality) from the Matrix and mix it with the rest of your 3-UC spirit energy. You become "whole." Therefore, I have suggested lately that we don't need to worry about all these different simultaneous incarnations we are involved in on Earth, or potential fire fragments left behind. Once we go through the Grid, we withdraw our participation in the Matrix simulation, and just like when we stop playing a computer game and turn off the computer, thus withdrawing all our energy from the game, we also withdraw all our energy from the Matrix when we exit. We have stopped "playing." There is nothing else to retrieve. We can now go on with our Orion business without having to be concerned about the Matrix anymore. I base this on what I have learned about this subject during the WPP sessions, but some of it more recently. The similarities between the Matrix and a computer game are sometimes stunning, and when we make that connection, things fall into place.

The only potential "concern" we might have is if we, after having exited through the Grid, still focus a lot of our attention on something we left behind in the Matrix. This means we never detached from it completely. In such cases, we will get help to come to terms with that.

What About the Animals? Can They Leave, too?

The more I've pondered this subject lately, it seems very plausible that the soul energy that animates animals is our *human* spirit energy. I think the Overlords use our human spirit fire to animate both animals and plants. You who have ever had pets know how loving and compassionate they are, and they also express empathy and try to comfort us. Even if we study lions, bears, and other ferocious predators in nature, by watching YouTube videos, for example, they might show an entire pride of lions in the wild running toward a human they recognize since years back, and start hugging and kissing, showing genuine love in such a way that we humans have even forgotten how to express to each other. These animal expressions are too profound to ignore, and much too similar to human traits to deny. Therefore, I think that even animal soul energy we have invested in animals and plants will return to the KHAA in the future, if things go well in the end. Even plants react to love and affection—there is consciousness there. I believe they, too, are hosted by human spirit fire.

Is it Possible to Become our True Self in the Matrix?

When we study people, we sometimes say to ourselves, "That person is authentic, but the one over there is not." However, what is authenticity, and how does that express itself in the Matrix?

Many people who have been subjected to a lot of trauma have an urge to be liked by *everyone*. They fear abandonment, rejection, not being good enough, being left alone, being ignored, treated as an outcast, and not being loved and accepted.

The more we become our "true selves," the less we care about being loved by *everyone*. When we are closer to ourselves, knowing ourselves to some degree, we are who we are, and we act accordingly without faking it. Some will like us the way we are, some will call us mad, others will ridicule us, and the list goes on. Our inner security and stability, however, prevents us from reacting to other people's ideas about us. It's *their* introject, and almost always, it is false. It has more to do with them than with us. Of course, we need each other, too, and interactions with others can uplift us and make us feel good (if we interact with non-toxic people, of course), but the more we heal, the less we are obsessed with what others think about us, and we don't randomly change because we notice some people don't like us the way we are.

But here is the catch: We can't truly be ourselves in this Matrix *because that requires full access to the genuine 3-UC*, and no one who is still residing here on Earth has that full access, or they would no longer be here. But by educating ourselves and exploring our inner sanctum, we reunite with an increasingly larger piece of our true self. Barely anything in our current personality is our true self—we are only more or less true to the individual we *want* to be in this construct in this lifetime. In Orion, we will not be the same person we are in this here and now. What we are at this moment is just the result of accumulated experiences in this particular lifetime, and the choices we've made. These experiences have formed a personality that is only relevant to *this* lifetime. If we would incarnate again, the person we are now would have ceased to exist shortly after you left that body. We start all over with a blank slate in a new lifetime, and the next personality will differ completely from the previous one. Therefore, when we reunite with our genuine 3-UC, the person I am now will just be one experience out of many. So, with the 3-UC, all our accumulated experiences in all earthly lifetimes, besides who we were before we got trapped here, will be our new personality in the KHAA. Who that individual will be depends on the summary of who we have been across our incarnations, and who you then decide to be. But I would argue that who you have become at the time you exit is a sign of your progress during your time in the Matrix. This last personality is your own final conclusion of you, based on all your Matrix experiences.

When you think everything seems hopeless, never forget who you truly are. You may not experience your full self yet because you need to exit first, but something magnificent and beautiful is waiting for you on the other side of the Grid—something we cannot fully appreciate in our current state.

Never forget what it means to be a creator god. We have a gift the Overlords have never had and never understood. Our problem is that we have forgotten we have this Divine Gift that makes us capable of creating with our imagination. For instance, did En.ki and the Overlords create this world? Only the blueprint—we created all that is still beautiful in this world, and many continue doing so, despite the decline in consciousness that is currently happening worldwide. But while plenty of us, knowingly or unknowingly, create beauty here, the Elite and the very physical, non-spirited, solid beings who run this world, actively and continually destroy much of what we have created. This makes us angry, sad, and even depressed. The surrounding beauty is demolished and replaced with concrete, machines, technology, and ugliness.

But despite what happens around us, we are not lesser creator gods now than we ever were. We need a few seconds between death and exiting through the Grid before we will regain our creative capacity in full.

Remember the above when you enter the astral. No one can touch you unless you let them. Don't give anyone in the astral your consent to *anything*, not even to speak with you.

12: Different Kinds of Humans

Human Biorobots and the Astral Circuit Boards

What most people probably don't think about is that our homo sapiens sapiens bodies are biorobots. Today, there is much talk about humans merging with the machine, becoming cyborgs. Yes, this is rapidly happening, but it's nothing new. We know En.ki reconstructed the Second Construct homo sapiens bodies when he isolated Earth and made it his own matrix. Still, the Second Construct also happened in a semi-physical density, not as solid as the Matrix, but still physical. It was probably more in line with life in other developing worlds. The lifespan was usually much longer, yet people died; we were still biorobots on the physical plane.

If this comes as a shock, and before we blame En.ki for this, it's nothing extraordinary if we think about it. We don't need to have bodies that are for more than bio-robotic when living in the physical universe. It's not much different from playing a computer game; the avatars in the game don't need to be biological to fill the purpose. Of course, En.ki limited our perspectives 96-fold, and he gave us amnesia and the recycling program, and that, in my opinion, are hideous crimes. But creating bio-robotic bodies, in general, is not. The Queen does that too, and so do other creator gods when they create new worlds in the physical realm. I would seriously argue that our brains, in the astral body, are a metaphysical circuit board, not very dissimilar from a computer circuit board, and this circuit board manifests as a physical brain in the 3-D sapiens body.

What is important is the consciousness that animates the physical bodies. The bodies themselves, in these lower realms, are just tools or vessels, making it possible to navigate through solid matter.

What the Overlords are doing now, however, is to upgrade (or I would say downgrade) our current bio-robotic bodies, so we can function in the Nanoverse (my alternative term for the Orion Universe). This is, of course, what is at the bottom of all this nanotechnology we hear about daily. So, when we talk about becoming cyborgs, it's not incorrect, but it would probably be more correct to say we're going from one bio-robotic body to another, which also is going to be "immortal." If something happens to those bodies, any organ can be exchanged easily with nanotechnology.

With this brief introduction in mind, we can dig into the different humans that are inhabiting the Earth. This is based on research, dot-plotting, and observation, and it might not be 100% correct in all the details, but I think it's overall accurate. Usually, we can't distinguish between these types of humans just by their looks—these types all host sapiens bodies like yours and mine. The difference is on another plane of existence.

List of Different Humans

Keeping in mind that this list might not be complete. I will mention the kinds I have stumbled upon, read about, and have discussed with the Orion source.

1. **3-UCs** (humans). To qualify as human, we must comprise soul, mind, and spirit body. In this matrix, most people are almost fully disconnected from their spirit body, however, and operate mostly on a soul-mind level, as 2-UCs. Those who operate on that level still qualify as humans because they possess Spirit, even though they might be disconnected.

2. **2-UC+ (2-UCs with access to Spirit)**. I put this category here, as well, though we can't know for sure whether there are such beings here. If there are, they might be difficult to distinguish from humans in the Matrix.

3. **2-UCs** (soul-minds without spirit body). These are Orion ETs who were hijacked by the Overlords when they came too close to Earth. The Overlords sucked them into a "syringe," and they were caught up in the recycling process like the rest of us. These are beings who developed in the physical realm but left their home world and became non-physical. They have yet to gain spirit in the KHAA, so they are still not creator gods.

4. **Artificial Souls** ("Non-Player Characters" [NPCs]). There are debates about what these beings really are and what animates them if they are not soul-minds. The following is my current view on

what they might be, based on logic gained from what we already know about Earth and the astral and have discussed thus far in this book. I would say that these sapiens bodies are animated by the artificial souls only. There are no 3-UCs (Players) investing their consciousness in these astral avatars (astral bodies). I suggest these sapiens are completely programmed to function as artificial humans. These artificial souls are incarnated here to create distractions and confusion. They are completely of the Matrix and can't function outside the Earth Grid. They *are* the astral body plus technological programming. Although we should not generalize, it's probably okay to suggest that most people who are extremely shallow seem to be able to speak on most subjects on a superficial level, and ridicule those who think outside the Matrix are NPCs. These are often the ones you can't have a spiritual conversation with because they will laugh at you and call you air-headed or something similar. They don't believe in an afterlife (properly so because they don't have one), and they can't look inward. They are extroverts, although, of course, far from all extroverts are NPCs. These beings are pre-programmed in the astral not to rebel against the System unless they are programmed to rebel. Therefore, the mundane, very physical person, and the Agent Smith type could be two sides of the same coin. What they have in common is that they are reliable—they follow the instructions the Overlords programmed them with, and the programmers know the NPCs will complete their mission as planned.

What about narcissists and psychopaths? Are they NPCs? Not necessarily, although some of them might be. I think psychology has it correctly for the most part when they tell us how narcissists are created, although they are still quite confused about the psychopaths, whether they were created in childhood or if it's genetic. What I have observed, from listening to psychologists, is that there is a certain percentage of narcissists and psychopaths that can't be explained away with traditional methods as a terrible childhood. In some cases, it seems the person was born that way.

This percentage *could* hypothetically be programmed NPCs. An example of this is all the school shootings. Most of those are executed identically, ending with the killers killing themselves not to be caught. Or perhaps they make sure the police shoot them because they shoot at the police.

The bottom line is that the NPCs are most likely programmed A.I. that the Overlords can make sentient enough to animate a body, or they are using random soul energy they have stored in the astral—energy they have programmed accordingly. It is completely possible for AI to run a biological machine like our physical sapiens bodies, but even though these NPCs can act just as convincing as genuine soul-minds, we recognize them because they lack inner insight and creative abilities. They are superficial, can be very intelligent, besserwissers, being able to talk on many subjects, and even reach top positions in organizations. But they have little to no imagination. Haven't we all met at least a few of those in our lives? I would argue there are a lot of these people around.

It's important, however, that we are careful with labeling people NPCs. I am confident there are humans who by now are so programmed through age-long manipulation that they think all that exists is what we can perceive with the five senses. The difference is that these humans might at least have some grasp that there *could* be something more than this reality, but they might not believe in it—they have become too solid and attached to this world over time.

1. **Cloned Beings.** We hear a lot about cloning, especially from whistleblowers who have been part of, or are still part of, the Secret Space Program (SSP). With technology, they can now create doppelgängers into which they can transfer the consciousness from the original human. This clone can then apparently function even outside the Dome, like the Greys, and perhaps the so-called

Reptilian Dracos, both being cyborgs, inhabited by Sirian and other ET races' 2-UCs. Within the SSP, it seems these clones are used temporarily when these so-called "Super Soldiers" are being hijacked and mind-controlled to go on a mission. When the mission is over, they are transferred back to the original body, while the clone is apparently put in stasis until "the next time." But then there are rumors, which seem to be true, that many prominent politicians and others have clones, too. These work differently because, in these cases, their original consciousness is not transferred. If the original person is still alive, the clone is used as a substitute for one reason or another. We saw Hillary Clinton's clone malfunction a few years ago, when her cloned body got a hiccup and started jerking, acting like a malfunctioning robot. Her guards were quick to get her into the car before she completely stopped working. That was on international TV. Something like this cloning technique could be used for NPCs, as well. After all, the Overlords have our Metaverse clones already made, ready to go, thanks to all the information we've shared online since the Internet started and we got smartphones, etc. It's more than likely that the Overlords can steal soul energy, program it, and put it into an artificial soul, i.e., a tailor-made astral body.

2. **The Global Elite and Their Bloodlines.** During my WPP years, I was told I should be grateful I am not of a pure Elite Bloodline because they will be the first to be disposed of. In the WPP, I discussed how En.ki, in the Second Construct, created the Brotherhood of the Snake, where snake stands for wisdom. He recruited the most intelligent humans around, and with his glib tongue, En.ki manipulated these humans to think they were special. So, he gave them knowledge about the Universe, and he handed them esoteric knowledge, such as "magic," i.e., how to tame and control energy, and how to manipulate other people's energy. These beings are like the Nazgûls in The Lord of the Rings—they are "immortal" but tormented, and they serve only one Master—En.ki. They are immortal in the sense that when they reincarnate, they don't go through the BLA, and therefore, they have most memories

intact when they reincarnate into the same bloodline. The rest their parents can fill in.

These pure Elite seed lines, if pure, are easy to possess (see Chapter 1). Therefore, Marduk and En.ki are very strict with keeping the Elite bloodlines pure, so they can be possessed by them, but also by others. And who are the others? They are the Sirians, the so-called "Nommos," whom I mentioned in the WPP. They were locked up by Khan En.lil inside the Black Sun in the Sirius star system after they had committed serious crimes, and they were stripped of their creative abilities and could only float around inside their prison aimlessly. These Sirians were En.ki's cohorts, and they were trapped in the beginning of the Third Construct—the Matrix. However, En.ki wanted them back, but he could not free them completely. Instead, he let these beings possess the Global Elite, using technology to accomplish this. So, these Elites high in the bloodline hierarchy are possessed by these Sirians. There is still a human 3-UC in there, but the Sirians have taken over their bodies, and they become so-called walk-ins, exactly in the same manner they plan to do with all of us in Metaverse. These Nommos are already riding human Avatars through the Top Elite. They can't take a human body, so they need a real human 3-UC hosting the body—or at least a 2-UC. Also, they are what we humans call demons. They are the Nommos, shapeshifting into form in the astral. This doesn't necessarily mean that Bill Gates, and those on his level, are Nommos, although some of them might be. I'm talking about higher in the hierarchy.

13: Short on Narcissism and Human Creativity

I would like to expand a little on narcissism, something I discussed in new terms and at some length in The ORION Book, Volume 1. But I also want to show how amazingly creative the human mind is—perhaps even more so in a little toddler, who tries to cope with a very harsh home environment.

In the previous book, we discussed how the traumatized and emotionally wounded toddler creates a false self as a coping mechanism, so the false self can take the beating and the verbal abuse from the caregivers, while the real self is hiding beneath the false persona that is slowly but surely developing. Thus, the real self stays in a toddler mode, while the false self becomes the only active personality who runs the show throughout the entire lifetime. This false self is who we call a narcissist.

Narcissism runs on a sliding scale. Only if the person scores the highest, which is 10 on the scale, psychologists can diagnose him or her with Narcissistic Personality Disorder (NPD). This means the false self, which the toddler created to protect himself or herself, has *completely* taken over the body, and the little child inside is literally asleep. However, let's say a person scores a 6 on the scale for narcissism, the narcissistic traits have taken over the genuine person by 60%, and so on.

In all the tragedy following narcissistic abuse, it's amazing how a child, from being a toddler to maybe five years old or so, can create this alter ego that is so strong that it engulfs the genuine being who was born into that body. But according to psychology, this is exactly what happens, and it makes sense.

From the time when the narcissistic false self is developed, the toddler, the little child, gets buried inside the body, letting the narcissistic thought form, if you will, take over the entire show. This false persona thinks they *are* the person, whereas it was created to protect the genuine person from abuse. This false self also spends its entire life trying to solve a mother issue the genuine soul suffered through at six to eighteen months, where they could not separate from their mother. So, the narcissistic false self goes into relationships, often romantic relationships, where the partner becomes the surrogate mother, whom the narcissist first gets attached to (love bombing in the beginning of the relationship), then needs to devalue (just like a toddler does with their "annoying" mother—a normal process in a child's development—and then they eventually discard the partner (unknowingly, they try to separate from the surrogate *mother*). However, this never resolves because the partner is not the actual mother, so the narcissist usually starts a new relationship, and the same pattern plays out. Thus, it goes on repeatedly throughout the narcissist's entire life.

I discussed all this in The ORION Book Volume 1, but I want to recap it here to refresh the reader's memory, which will be helpful while we can discuss another issue.

A narcissist is our mirror—the opposite of us. It gets interesting when they try to heal, even so little. If you and I start our inner healing process, and it's done correctly, we feel better and better, and stronger and stronger, more secure within ourselves, and we set up boundaries, because we now value ourselves. This is a normal process for a regular person who has gone through trauma in their lives.

Not so with a narcissist. If a narcissist goes to therapy, the therapist is not healing the dormant child, i.e., the genuine person within, but they unwittingly try to heal the narcissist if they don't know what they're doing (which unfortunately is the case with many therapists, even according to Prof. Vaknin). It's well known that narcissists don't make progress in therapy, and there is a reason for this. Every time they confront something inside themselves which is supposed to heal them, they feel they're dying. It's the exact opposite of a regular person. The narcissists often say they have no "core," there is no core being inside them—only a huge black hole, like a void. Therefore, every time you remove something from the narcissists, it becomes less of them. It's like pealing an onion, but when you get to the core of the onion, there is no core, and the onion is no more. A therapist who is not highly educated in narcissism makes them peel off everything there is of the narcissist, and if the narcissist would finish the therapy, he or she literally dies because it's a false persona. I would say narcissists are very much "alive" thought forms who can think for themselves. Indeed, they can be extremely intelligent sometimes, but they don't respond to treatment because they feel the therapist is killing them. So, they, as time progresses in therapy, cease to exist—literally—and they panic. Therefore, they resist change. Change means death to them. They are programs, having a task, a mission, and that's all there is to it. Their job is to protect the inner child from abuse that may no longer exist. The narcissist is frozen in time somewhere in childhood.

To look at this more virtually, the narcissists' false persona was born about two to three years into the person's life—in one of the child's most important developmental stage. The narcissist was not there when the baby was born. But it replaced the baby's mind, so if the narcissists go through therapy, they can't go further back than, let's say, to the age of two or three. Before that, they did not exist. Therefore, it's impossible for the narcissists' personae to survive death and reincarnate because they are not the person; they are just "fluff" that will most likely disperse when the body dies.

Feeling Sorry for the Narcissist

It is very common to feel sorry for the narcissists, even though they have tortured us and deprived us of our lives and our own personality. If we leave them, we often give in to their drama, and we feel bad for leaving them, or we empathize with what seems to be a vulnerable person beneath all that abuse.

I included this chapter for one reason, and that is to convey important information to the reader if you are, or have been, in a situation when you had to separate from a narcissist. We must remember that the narcissist is *not* a person; it's a coping mechanism who most likely cannot survive body death. Instead, when the narcissist's body dies, the genuine toddler inside, who never developed into an adult human, now leaves the body, as usual, and gets recycled again, hopefully to a better life. So, death is the only thing that can free the genuine soul buried deep inside the person. No therapy can reach them because of the narcissistic overlay who defends the inner child ferociously—they are a complicated coping mechanism, that is very mechanical, and like Sam Vaknin says, he is more A.I. than a real person (he was diagnosed with narcissism twice)[[55]].

So, the one we should feel empathy for is not the "thought form" that is the narcissist but the horribly abused little toddler inside, who is hiding and never developed. That is the *genuine* tragedy. The thought form is nothing but a malignant overlay that can't distinguish between good and evil, thinking everybody is out to get him or her, having no genuine soul on their own, unable to feel empathy, compassion, and love—other than when they mimic these three human characteristics to gain soul energy, so the thought form can survive (research "thought form" and you will see the eerie connection to narcissism). The narcissist develops into what they become because of people around him. They study us with a magnifying glass and learn everything about us, so they know how to behave and can use our own traits against us to get the loosh (soul energy) they so much need to stay alive. Narcissists can't survive without feeding on others because they can't produce their own energy, obviously—they are not truly sentient. They are a split personality of the original child—a division of the mind of a terrified toddler—a personality that went its own way, having its own thinking processes, developed by copying what other people think and do to use that against them. Thus, they can be very convincing and take on any persona they think is relevant to a certain life situation. Therefore, they fool most people. They develop intelligence and cold empathy out of necessity to survive in what they consider a hostile environment, where no one can be trusted, and everyone is an enemy. They live with constant paranoia.

As you, the reader, can imagine now, there is nothing you can do for the narcissist. All you can do is to save yourself—the sooner the better, and if we want to empathize, it is the inner child who needs the empathy and the compassion, not the narcissistic, malignant coping mechanism.

14. The Harvesting of Souls

Warning! This Chapter is not for the Faint-Hearted!

For years, I have excluded the following information from my regular public exposes because it's quite disturbing. However, eventually people need to know this, and I think it's time to bring this up. It is about the harvesting of souls, as the chapter title shows, and it's *nothing* like we have been taught it is. It is much more sinister. All this information developed from discussions with the Orion source back in the days.

What Does Harvesting Imply?

In New Age circles, and according to many channeled materials, the Harvest is an ascension process. Those who have gained a certain level of awareness or a significant increase in consciousness will ascend to the Fourth or the Fifth Dimension. Sometimes, as with the famous RA Material (Law of One), the channeled entities are here to help us humans in the Harvest process. To those engaged in this belief, it may sound quite benevolent and uplifting. It takes you out of the reincarnation cycle, and you are to experience something loftier and more inspiring. This is, of course, why many people fall for this. Those who have read the WPP, however, and have taken the information to heart, know that the Ascension Program is En.ki's program that supposedly will help us graduate and leave the Matrix—even if it takes millions of years, according to the RA people.

But what if the entire Harvest process is one gigantic trap? This is exactly what it is if we are to believe the Orion source. Let's investigate what he and I discussed approximately ten years ago.

The Extraterrestrial "Gold Rush"

I became familiar with the ancient "Anunnaki" Gold Rush by reading Zecharia Sitchin's book, "The Twelfth Planet," many years ago. In his translations of the Sumerian texts, he wrote that the early homo sapiens, after replacing Anunnaki miners, were mining gold for the Overlords. The story goes the gods needed the gold for digestion and longevity, but also for their Nibiru atmosphere as a shield.

According to my Contact, this is a major fabrication, or a mistranslation and interpretation, at best. The "gold" in the texts doesn't refer to mining or to gold at all—it is about crops, such as wheat, although these are metaphors. What the gods wanted, and still want, is to yield crops, which is the metaphor for humans. What do humans do when the crops are ripe? We harvest the best ones and discard the bad ones.

Thus, where the gods are concerned, the gold being mined is humans with the "tastiest blood." By "tastiest blood," I refer to blood as the life force in the body. It pertains to the soul and soul energy. When it's time for the harvest of humans, the Overlords are getting prepared for a feast in soul energy. In other words, they will eat us (even the Pleiadians were discussing this in Marciniak's books in the 1990s).

But they won't eat all of us because the gods are picky. They want to feast on those who are more "evolved" than others and have increased their consciousness during their lifetime.

What is the Fifth Dimension People Talk About?

So many people in the alternative communities, such as New Age, and others, believe they are going to ascend to the Fifth Dimension after death, and some of them believe they will ascend while still alive[[56]]. Unfortunately, things are not what they believe they are. The gods want to eat these souls once they depart from their bodies. The more raised in consciousness a person is, the more galactic current they create, according to the Orion source, and the more they create, the more food for the gods. Behind the orchestration of the Harvests are the Khan Kings. Harvesting does not happen all the time; it's restricted to galactic "seasons," when the galactic waves are in favor of making people wake up. Such a Harvest is apparently due now, after the nanosecond happened between 1987-2012, when the cosmic winds from the Galactic Center hit the Earth Grid.

So, it's not a good idea to be a New Ager, reaching for the Fifth Dimension. Some of these souls will get eaten.

Humans Harvesting Humans

So far, we have talked about the Sirians and channeled entities being behind the Harvests, but there is another aspect of it, as well. We are also dealing with treacherous humans, who help the Overlords to harvest other humans, very much knowing what they are doing. These are the gurus and the prominent spiritual teachers of the world. They are here on a mission to accrue followers whom the Overlords then can harvest and eat. These gurus and teachers have been promised great rewards after their own lives are over (knowing the Overlords, I would not be surprised if they are being eaten, too, unbeknownst to them).

It always rubbed me the wrong way, checking out these gurus and teachers, noticing what was going on under the surface. Every time I've looked, I found crimes. Some were rapists, others were stealing money from their followers, and yet others were pedophiles, wife murderers, and the list goes on. All this is covered up by a holy and enlightened façade. There we have the real criminals in the spiritual field. Of course, among these are the actual gurus, East Indians, and others, but also many western teachers, who turn out to be, when we dig a little deeper, con artists, malignant narcissists, or worse. It's sometimes quite shocking but might not come as a surprise.

The gods use galactic currents, precession of equinoxes, and ethical behavior to yield the best crops. The crops considered undesirable will be destroyed and mixed, as usual, with soul fires from other departed souls, and sent back to Earth. They will be mixed out, or as reapers call it, "crop self-correction." Up until now, at least, and after previous Harvests, the ones sent back to Earth were again put into the System, and maybe when the next Harvest happened, they too were ripe enough to be eaten. And like it says in the RA Material, not all Harvests were "fruitful." There were Harvests in the past where no souls were harvested because of lack of spiritual awareness.

Conclusion

What does it mean to be eaten, compared to having the artificial soul (the astral body) destroyed? It sounds like the same thing. Not exactly, though. We have already discussed the procedure of what happens to a regular person after death, unless they exit through the Grid: They will have their astral body, containing their soul fire, destroyed, and mixed with other people's soul fires. Then they will get another avatar/astral body and be shot back into a new meat body on Earth, starting over from scratch.

As I understand it, when a soul is eaten, the Overlords "open" the astral body and suck out the soul fires, figuratively speaking, and mix with their own fires. Thus, they gain soul energy. These fires will never be molded into a new avatar again.

This simply means that the 3-UC, who invested their consciousness into that astral body now has their artificial soul fires eaten—no more incarnations, as I understand it. This will, of course, not destroy the 3-UC, but it seems that particular 3-UC can no longer incarnate in the Matrix System. What will happen after that is unknown to me at this point.

How does this apply to us who are on our unique journey, going through the Grid? Will we also be eaten? Would we not be some of the tastiest souls there are? Probably, but that doesn't mean we are going to let that happen. Everything we've been rehearsing regarding exiting through the Grid is still as valid as ever. No one, Overlord or no Overlord, can interfere with our intentions and our freewill. As we've discussed hundreds of times, all we need to do is to exit through a hole in the Grid. For those who are unfamiliar with how to exit, go to *https://wespenrevideos.com/* and click on "EXITING THE GRID" in the top section and start reading and listening to the videos. It's crucial that you do!

I would say we are all safe, but only if we choose to exit after this lifetime. If we don't, we could be in trouble. The bottom line is that those who get eaten are being eaten because of their ignorance. Those who work on ascending are the ones who are tricked because they know not what they are doing. We do!

This may all sound horrific, but I need to let people know. Knowledge is always better than ignorance because we can plan. And plan we must. We need to get rid of all attachments to the Matrix before we die, so nothing tempts us to come back. And to be honest, we might not come back to Earth even if we wanted to, with the information in this chapter in mind. It seems none of us is the subject to another reincarnation cycle, no matter what.

15. The Use of Cosmic Energy

Energy, the Building Block of Creation

Everything is energy. There is nothing in the Universe, Matrix, or Orion that is not of energy. All from the most solid object to the most ethereal is energy. Energy can run free and untamed, as it does in the Cosmic water (the VOID), or it can be tamed and controlled, as we do when we isolate energy to flow in a Direct Current (DC) or an Alternate Current (AC).

We often separate between the material universe and the Spirit Universe, the latter being all that is *not* the material universe. This is only a perspective, however, because ultimately, even the material universe is the Spirit Universe. Another thing often discussed are dimensions and densities. If we want to discuss it in the broadest sense, there are innumerous dimensions and densities, from the highest and most purely ethereal level of Orion, and down to the most solid level of matter there is. However, we rarely look at it that way; we tend to separate these different levels by grouping them into smaller groups. For example, we might talk about the Spirit Universe, the KHAA, as having one group of dimensions and densities, and the physical universe has its own dimensions and densities. Even the Matrix, with its encapsulated astral realm, also has its own dimensions and densities. This is, of course, arbitrary, and only something we humans have come up with, trying to avoid confusion and get organized, so people use the same terms, and we can hopefully understand each other.

What separates different dimensions and densities, whether we discuss the KHAA or the material realm, is the vibration and the frequency range. It's impossible to say exactly where one dimension or density stops and another one starts. In metaphysics, we usually think of these fuzzy boundaries as characteristic. We might call it an additional dimension when a new type of outstanding characteristic adds to the previous level. Dimensions are, per definition, just perspectives, and viewpoints, i.e., points from which we view something—different "angles," if you wish. It doesn't need to be physical perspectives, and usually it is not. It's happening inside our minds. As mentioned, all is arbitrary and are just labels we have put on different frequential perspectives. Thus, Albert Einstein said to the effect, *one can't solve a problem from the same level it was created*. What he meant was that your thoughts need to vibrate higher than the thoughts with which the problem was created in order to solve it. We call our Matrix frequency of "visible light" the *Third Dimension*. Within this Third Dimension, we have almost infinite densities, i.e., solidities. For instance, a table is more solid than a dust bowl. They are of different densities. Sometimes, the differences in density could be greater than that, so we might not see a certain object on a level where the molecules are few, with lots of space between.

Now, we can better see how creation works—both on our 3-D level, and as far out in the KHAA imaginable. It's just a matter of how solid things are, and in the KHAA, where matter is not present, it's more about which frequency (vibration) we create inside our minds. This vibration we can then manifest in the KHAA in form of a creation. This inner creation corresponds to the vibration of our outer manifestation. This determines which dimension our mind's creation will manifest. A skilled creator god knows exactly in what dimension their creation will manifest before it is manifested because just like a musician knows which note to play because of its vibration, the creator god becomes familiar with vibrations and frequencies (dimensions) over "time." In the Cosmic Water, we change the waveforms according to the vibrations of our thoughts. In the physical worlds, technology is used to manifest ideas and images inside the creator god's mind to make the creation as solid as they intend it to be and stay that way. With technical equipment, sound waves are used to create shapes and forms and keep them within the range of the solidity being envisioned. Thus, we have galaxies, stars, planets, and the rest of what we call the physical universe. The so-called Dark Matter may comprise two separate things, as I understand it:

1) Even the physical universe exists in the KHAA, e.g., a certain galaxy we can see in a telescope is only a part of the galaxy that happens to be in the visible light spectrum. But the galaxy exists across other spectra of the electromagnetic diagram, and we can only see 4% of it. Thus, the "4% Universe," as I have discussed many times. The range of the electromagnetic spectrum we use here on Earth stretches from ultraviolet to infrared, but there are many more spectra we don't yet know about.

2) A creator god creates solely in the Spirit Universe, rather than in the physical realm. These creations only exist within certain frequencies (dimensions) in the Spiritual realm. This is only partly true, however, because I have seen indicators that what we call planets are just sun/stars within the KHAA that manifest as planets in the physical realm.

Creating with Freewill

Creation is all about taming and controlling energy. The more chaos inside our minds, the more chaos we create around us, and vice versa. Hence, creation can be beneficial and benevolent, or it can be non-beneficial and malevolent, depending on the creator and his or her intentions. Thus, we have a universe of freewill. This doesn't mean we can't set up rules to avoid unpleasant creations because that is also a part of freewill. Then the malignant creators can choose whether to abide or break the rules, which again is a part of freewill. But in a freewill universe, *freewill comes with responsibility*. A creator can, of course, choose not to take responsibility, which happens both on Earth and elsewhere, but then there are consequences, until creators either learn that, in the long run, it's more pleasant to create benevolently, because we eventually reap what we sow. They may learn the consequences become too dire, but that could take a long time for some beings to accept. Not because of karma, but because of consequences of the effects they create. Sometimes, they get away with it, and sometimes not.

Freedom of Creation in a Freewill Universe

We can easily see in the visible universe that stars have different densities. Astronomers know this, of course, and the color of a particular star determines its density. And the frequency within which the star vibrates from sound waves determines the density of the entire developing world the particular creator god has created. Within that density range, an experiment with a new star race, or races, can be produced, leading to new universal experiences.

In the KHAA, other creator gods, who have access and prefer to create there, develop their own worlds in these dimensions, and these worlds are purely etheric in nature, such as Tiamat once was before it fell into matter after the Titan War.

Thus, all beings in the Universe use energy in different ways, but all beings use it. When something is chaotic, the energy is not tamed, and when it's organized, it's tamed and structured.

Entropy

Another term for the relation between chaos and order, often used in physics, is *entropy*. The higher the entropy, the higher the level of chaos and disorder. Therefore, we say that the more organized we become, and the more we learn, the more we lower the entropy. We can use this term in metaphysics to denote whether a person is increasing or decreasing in awareness. We could say, for example, that "Sara made a few great choices that significantly lowered her entropy."

Energy and Magick

When we talk about magick, we often distinguish between white and black magick[[57]]. All magick is just about skills in taming and using energy to one's benefit and according to one's intentions. There is nothing supernatural about it. Controlling energy is normal practice in the Universe. It all equates to how skilled the practitioner is in using it. Therefore, the only difference between white and black magick is the intention behind it, and the desired outcome in theory and practice. There are religious people, particularly within Christianity, who condemn all kinds of magick, saying it's of the Devil. By doing this, they say it's a sin to create. What we call magick is just a higher form of creation within the Matrix—an attempt to become a creator god while still living in the simulation. By that, I don't mean everybody should now start practicing ritual magick the way Crowley or other magicians did. What I'm saying is that magick is just imagination, intentions, and the usage of energy to fulfill a purpose. Then it depends on the practitioner what the outcome will be. It is never a good idea to call up deities and demons from the astral, which is common practice in ritual magick.

Astrology and Destiny

It matters when we are born because that predestines us in *this* lifetime. It matters where the celestial bodies are located at birth because these are the energies we have downloaded into our bodies when we leave the womb. We get our traits, our talents, and our capabilities in general from a set of astrological configurations. Most people, unwittingly, think they control their own destiny, i.e., their lives, when they, for the most part, do not. It requires both courage and determination to break our predestined lives (something some of us are doing right now). As we all know, it's not easy, and there are consequences. But we also all know that it's worth it.

16. The Misuse of Cosmic Energy

Where Does the Orion Universe Start and End?

The center of the Milky Way Galaxy is also known by two other names, the "Womb of the Mother" and the "Central Fire." These terms come from the Pleiadians and the Orion source, respectively. Both mean the same thing; it is the place from where Spirit Fire emanates. Does this mean it's the Pleroma? I can't say either way, but I personally don't think the Galactic Center is the Pleroma. I feel confident the Pleroma surrounds us all the time, and that the Orion Universe is just an encapsulated part of the overall Pleroma—a boundary.

Here is a question to ponder: If the center of the Milky Way Galaxy is the Central Fire, what does that make the rest of the galaxies, such as the Andromeda, etc.? Is the Milky Way equivalent to the Orion Universe, and the other galaxies are external universes? That is something to investigate. I am pondering this because I have been told the Central Fire is in the center of the Universe. That suggests that our galaxy, the Milky Way, is the Orion Universe. It also means, based on what I was told, and if my assumption is correct, soul-minds cannot travel to the Andromeda galaxy, or any other galaxy, because if those are other universes, they follow completely different laws and rules, and they are not freewill universes. The way we are constructed, we would perish there.

If we think about it, the way the Orion source described universes was like lilies in a pond (galaxies in the Cosmic Water?)[[58]]. They come in clusters of twelve, and then in another cluster of twelve, and so on. And Sophia, as pure Spirit, is number thirteen—the Creatrix and Senior Overseer, her being what is within the universes and what is in between them (all of it being the Pleroma). It starts making sense, and it's coming to me as a stream of consciousness as I write this. It doesn't mean it's necessarily correct because of that, but more often than not, when this happens, it tends to add up.

I will try to investigate this some more, however. I've suggested this before, but it's just a loose idea so far; something to ponder. I know the

RA entities had a difficult time discussing galaxies with the channeling team because they thought of galaxies as universes.

Energy Theft

Until recently, the Central Fire was used to boost this Matrix, unbeknownst to us humans. The Overlords and the Elite stole this energy from us because they themselves can't draw energy from the Galactic Center anymore and must therefore do it through us. Normally, and as an evolving species, we are allowed to keep the energy within the system until we are evolved enough to contribute to the overall universe.

A little bit of recap: While evolving on a planet or in a star, the soul energy is a loan, and star races pay back their "debt" when they leave the developing world where they were born. But in our case, it's misused because we give it away to the Overlords, and more and more energy was consumed as time went by. Other star races complained about this because it escalated, and the Overlords also used (and are still using) this energy for their own space travels and space wars with other star races. Our energy also helps them create portals and stargates to other star systems—not to mention they suck us dry of our energy to boost their own, which has been on decline almost since the dawn of the Matrix. So, we unwittingly help the Overlords run amok, not only here but also in other star systems. This is not how the Central Fire was meant to be used.

Therefore, it was requested that this must stop because it affects other parts of the Universe—not only our neck of the galaxy. Thus, Orion wanted to strangle our access to the Central Fire, and we had to do with what we have—mainly to smoke the Overlords out. I believe this is part of the "Ultimatum" Orion gave the Overlords. They thought they had all the time in the world to complete their mission (to attack Orion), but now they lose "oxygen," i.e., soul and spirit fire, and they must hurry because they (and we) are running out of energy. Perhaps Orion is hoping the Overlords will attack prematurely with a weak army that Orion can easily defeat with only a few casualties, rather than waiting for them to build a huge armada of 3-UCs.

Anyway, the Queen loves us (her children), and she has been a little biased toward us, according to other Orion star races, since she gave us one more boost of energy (the nanosecond), as a last chance for us to wake up and leave. But in general, it did not help. Instead, the Overlords stole that as well, and we got very little of it. Also, the depletion of energy influences the Grid, which becomes thinner and thinner the less energy we have inside this construct, and this also creates holes in the energy net—the Grid becomes weaker with less energy to feed it. I think that was also a part of Orion's plan. It will make it easier for us to exit. Also, the battle between Orion and the Khan Kings in 2008-2009, amidst the nano-second, punches huge holes in the Grid, which let the Central Fire pour into the Matrix while we were still aligned with the Galactic Center[[59]]. Thus, we humans have received help from Orion more than once, but we have not been up to the task to recognize it, except for a small group of people, relatively speaking.

Now the Overlords are desperate because humans are starved of soul energy, and subsequently, so are the gods. Hence, we humans steal energy from each other, unwittingly in many cases, because it's not just narcissists who steal soul energy anymore—even "good people" do it without being aware of it. And the Overlords enjoy when we steal each other's energy because it ultimately becomes food for them, and they are glad to "help." This is what happens in social media, where people are drawing energy from each other, and this world becomes more and more narcissistic, which the Overlords want. In other words, we become more and more like them, and therefore, they will have an easier time taking us over in the final attack on Orion, explained in The ORION Book, Volume 1. Everything adds up.

Some of us wake up anyway, but we soon notice it's not a simple task. Yet, it's the only path we know of on which we can save ourselves. We reconnect with Spirit as we progress, as our minds stretch outside the Matrix, and we use this connection to liberate ourselves. Hence, we can still retrieve some fire from the Galactic Center. But the Matrix now takes so much energy that our own "batteries" run out nonetheless, and we may often feel exhausted and fatigued "for no reason."

Traumatized Into Obedience

The scientist, Harald Kautz Vella, gives us a profound understanding of A.I., the Singularity, Metaverse, and what is going on today[[60]]. I think his perspective is accurate, and it also shows how energy can be misused.

There seems to be more narcissistic abuse going on today than ever before in modern times. To some extent, it is probably because there are more people on the planet, but the abuse we experience today does not seem in proportion to that in the past. Many blame social media, and I agree social media creates a lot of narcissism and abuse. In this book, we have discussed that the Overlords want us to become like them, so they can easily take over our minds before they take over our spirit bodies, and that is true. However, another thing Mr. Vella is bringing up is that the Overlords want us traumatized because, as he explains, traumatized people run on *mental* personalities (the subconscious and unconscious mind). He says the mental field is linear, and therefore, quite predictable. It's stimulus-response: You say or do something, and you get a predictable counter-reaction that is sub- or unconscious. But emotionally, spiritually oriented people are not linear, and therefore unpredictable. Those who are emotionally and spiritually inclined, therefore, cannot be easily controlled by a computer system. Hence, the Overlords' goal is to traumatize us as much as possible, so we become reactive and predictable instead of spiritually unpredictable. Once people are in Metaverse, and thus, in the Cloud, it's important that the Elite and the Overlords can easily control all those people's minds to create a hive mind.

Sentient World Simulation (SWS) is a relatively new term that explains in more detail what Vella has said. SWS is an effort to model every person digitally to gain predictability to stimuli that can be used to control people's behavior[[61]]. So, *try to stay level-headed and don't engage in reactive behavior*. We, who want to leave this mind-controlled planet, must ourselves break loose from the mind control, and we do that by controlling our reactive behavior and exchange our uncontrolled reactions with controlled behavior that does not feed the System. Make sure you keep your unpredictable behavior. I've mentioned it before, but the Pleiadians said the same thing:

The Controllers have a difficult time controlling us because we are unpredictable.

Let's keep it that way.

Our Effects on the KHAA Once We're There

I have brought this up before, but it's worth discussing again to investigate this subject from a different angle.

As mentioned earlier, many star races in Orion are concerned about letting us out in the KHAA. They think we, as a soul group, are too much like the Overlords. I can completely see it from their perspective. A raw, unprepared human soul group out in the KHAA would be extremely dangerous and devastating for the entire Universe. Orion has enough problems with a certain number of star races, leaving the developing worlds and starting their journey into the KHAA. Among those are warlike races that run amok in the lower dimensions of the KHAA. Although they technically don't have access to the upper dimensions, their behavior has a ripple effect on the waves of the Cosmic Ocean. Thus, what happens in the lower regions also tends to affect the upper regions to some degree. So, this has become a problem.

Now take what we just discussed into perspective. The upper regions are still populated with ethical and benevolent creator gods, but what would happen if they let the human soul group out in its current shape? Well, it's not rocket science. We are creator gods by nature, so we will have access to the entire KHAA, and we can therefore create wherever we like. Then consider that we, as a soul group, are not very ethical and often refuse to take responsibility for our own actions, which we blame on others. If beings with such mentality started creating wildly in the KHAA, the wild west of the lower regions—the wars and conflicts—would now move into the upper dimensions of the KHAA, as well. When that happens, what will be the solution? To shut down the entire Universe and start all over? Possibly. Or maybe the Queen thinks a universe of freewill does not work, and she doesn't bother to create a new one? Even more possible. Perhaps she will uncreate the entire Milky Way Galaxy?

Putting all this in perspective makes it easier to understand why Orion is reluctant to let humanity out. Just opening the cage is not an option, in my opinion. But if Orion still chooses to do that, humankind must be contained somewhere else so this soul group does not create harm. In that containment, they must continue evolving until they become peaceful and ready to fly on their own. In other words, humankind must still be contained, whatever happens. The only difference is that there will be no Overlords trying to suppress their development. It might be a slow process for the soul group to recover and build ethical and moral strength and thus be willing to take full responsibility for themselves. None of us is perfect, for sure, but we can work on ourselves to the best of our ability. Because of the Law of Freewill, the human soul group, in its new containment, would need to evolve on their own. Otherwise, Orion breaks a secondary law, the Law of Non-Interference. Each soul group in the Universe must evolve on their own—that's part of the essential plan for this universe—it's built into its foundation.

All this applies to us, too, who are determined to leave. Think of yourself the way you are today when you read this. Who are you as a being? Are you aggressive? Defensive? Are you responsible? Compassionate? Ethical? Empathetic? Loving? Ponder these things and write down things you believe you need to improve and work on them. It's imperative that we enter the KHAA as the best possible version of ourselves. There is always room for improvement. Being creators in the KHAA does not include creating cool warlike computer games. This is also why it's a good idea to live our lives here on Earth until the end, using the remaining years to improve.

Some people ask me why we can't just commit suicide. There is more than one reason for this, but doing inner work during the rest of our lives is a reason as good as any not to end our lives prematurely.

Consequences of Misusing Energies in 3-D

We humans have misused our energy in the Matrix. Wittingly and unwittingly, we are helping the Overlords achieve their goals; us being the enthusiastic executioners of our own downfall. The spirit energy invested in this experiment was a loan, and now the Queen wants the energy back. That is the Ultimatum. The Overlords are desperate; they had a Plan A but no

Plan B, thinking they had all the time in the world to prepare for the invasion of Orion. To show they are serious, Orion now refuses to lend any more energy from the Central Fire to this construct, and that is what makes the Overlords desperate. They feel they will lose the race unless they speed up their entire process. That's what we see happening in the world today. The race is on, and things are implemented upon us at a baffling speed.

This was also what the Khan Kings' collaboration with LPG-C was about. The Overlords tried to create a Plan B, which included an agreement with the human soul group to cooperate with them, so Orion can't get to us. And Dr. Bordon fell right into the trap. Presenting himself as a "representative for humankind," he set us all up for signing a contract with the Devil—the Khans. To them, having someone presenting themselves as a representative is enough because Bordon then speaks for the entire soul group. Therefore, the Orion source was not in favor of Dr. A.R. Bordon. What right did Bordon have to speak for all humans? he said. Did he ask us what we really want? No, he didn't. This plan failed, and Bordon died, but he almost signed over humankind to the Khan Kings, thinking the Khans were "good people" with our interests in mind.

The reason there are currently so many people on the planet is because the Overlords need a lot of fire to put into the Cloud. Fire is sparse these days, and it needs to be conserved as fast as possible, so the gods have enough to invade Orion. However, now it seems they have the energy they need, and therefore, they can let people die off, reducing us to a number they ultimately can handle, which is about 3% of the current population. That's the number of cyborgs they need for the Invasion. They may leave the rest of us to perish, which might be a "good thing." People who don't want to go into Metaverse can build their own communities, and when they die, they can potentially leave the Matrix because the current Grid will, at that point, probably not exist anymore, replaced by the A.I. Cloud.

Repentance of the "Good Guy"

It seems like, with a few exceptions, this world is composed of abusers and codependents, whether it's in romantic relationships or the relation to governments and other authorities. This is very interesting when it comes to energy consumption because who is the "good guy" and who is the "bad guy," or are both the abuser and the codependent bad? Yes, they are, and they continue being so until they repent.

What do I mean by this? Well, let's take a classical example: When a codependent leaves their narcissist, or the narcissist leaves them, the codependent complains about how much they gave in the relationship, but they got nothing back, except abuse and neglect. This is usually true, but from a cosmic perspective, what was the codependent actually doing during the relationship? They borrowed energy from the Central Fire, and instead of using it constructively, they gave it to the narcissist in hope to improve the relationship, and the narcissist gratefully accepted it and consequently used it to boost themselves, but also to use it against the codependent to abuse them even more. So, the codependent, who thinks it's his or her fault, borrows more energy from the cosmos and gives it to the narcissist, who now can abuse even more.

This becomes increasingly significant when we talk about the Overlords, to whom the entire population is codependent. Human 3-UCs have, over time, sucked in an overwhelming amount of energy from the Central Fire into the Matrix system and given it most of this energy to the Overlords. The Overlords take some of it as loosh, and the rest they use to feed the System, so they can oppress us even more. We run out of energy, so we borrow more fire from the Cosmos and give it to our oppressors, who then can oppress us even more, and so it continues. The bottom line is that the codependents, who think they are good people, are actually the ones who are stealing the energy from the Universe and invest it in their own oppressive system to feed those who oppress us, while they themselves go without.

Of course, this would not happen without the Overlords, but if we look at this soberly, and the way Orion looks at it, we are the ones who are feeding the System and are creating the imbalance in universal energy. Therefore, we are guilty of misusing energy until we wake up and repent and are willing to stop our destructive ways. We must disconnect from our local narcissist, as well as with the Overlords, and then the entire Matrix, or we will be redeemable and judged together with the Overlords.[62]

I hope the reader understands how crucial it is that we work on ourselves. If someone is together with a narcissist, they'd better start working on taking appropriate steps to disconnect. Otherwise, they are accomplices, and even instigators of increasing the energy debt that is piled upon the rest of humanity. I would go so far as to say the reason why people don't wake up, so we all can leave, is because the majority of the population refuses to see the codependent situation they are in, and if they do, they refuse to do something about it. It is not a benevolent thing to be a codependent.

Afterthoughts on Use and Misuse of Energy

I have briefly mentioned researcher Billy Carson earlier in this book, but there is another thing he's talked about on TikTok that also goes hand in hand with what I have conveyed over the years, and that has to do with crystals and their usefulness.

People buy crystals because they think they're beautiful, or they think they have some magic power. Well, they have power, although it's hardly magical. Crystals, particularly those that are double terminated, are powerful communication devices and storages of memory. Extraterrestrials who visit here use them for both those purposes. The crystals help them remember who they are, despite the veil of forgetfulness that shrouds this planet. They can also use them to communicate with the KHAA. A person using crystals for these reasons must, of course, first know how to program them, which is something I am not familiar with.

It is interesting that there are "crystal forests" inside the Earth. I would argue they are there to store memories of everything that happens on planet Earth—it's perhaps the Akashic Records so many people talk about. Maybe these records are not located in the astral, but underground. I would also suggest that with the right training, we can tune into these crystal forests and might find the answer to everything that has happened on Earth since it was created and up to date. Billy Carson discusses multidimensional crystals, and more, in one of his videos. He also brings up the nano world in the same way I have done[[63]].

And speaking of memories. It seems like more and more people who are waking up are becoming more forgetful than before. Most of us perhaps imagined it would be the opposite. However, I'm talking about short-term memory, not the long-term. We tend to forget more things the more awareness we get. Why is that?

I think it is because Earth is getting denser because of all the abuse going on here, with the manipulation that is beyond imagination right now. That's a very low frequency. Those who are waking up, however, are going in the opposite direction—we are getting less dense and more ethereal. Therefore, the chasm between our soaring awareness and the world around us is getting wider, and it becomes more difficult to interact with the dense physical world. We detach and disconnect more and more all the time. Still, we must interact with the physical world, too, to some extent, but we become more forgetful because our focus is mostly not on the physical world. I have noticed the effects of this myself, and it would be interesting to hear about other people's experiences. If you are on my forum at wespenreboards.com/, you can comment on it there, or you can do it in one of the comment sections on my blog at wespenrevideos.com/.

17. A few Notes on Evolution

There is another advantage we humans have before other star races. We have high awareness. I have been told we can evolve in a thousand years what it takes other star races millions of years in comparison. This comes not only from the Orion source, but was something I heard for the first time from Barbara Marciniak's Pleiadians. So, there are two separate sources, completely independent from each other, saying the same thing. With this in mind, we can imagine how hard the Overlords must work to keep us under wraps. There is a great metaphor explaining this, and I don't remember where I read it, but it goes like this: Think of us humans as balloons at the bottom of a pool. The Overlords must constantly force the balloons to stay under water because if they cannot control the balloons for just a split second, they float up to the surface.

Always Put Yourself First!

It's crucial that we put ourselves before others. People who have not particularly followed my work that much might gasp at this statement, thinking that it's always more important to be of service to others. I understand that because that's how we've been brainwashed to believe. Not by the government or the media, necessarily, but from these tricky beings whom well-meaning people channel from within the astral. They are quick to teach us we need to be Service to Others (STO) more often than being Service to Self (STS.) Otherwise, we won't ascend to these amazing higher dimensions (where the gods will eat our soul energy).

With the understanding I have today, reading the RA Material and other channeled messages promoting STO, I see a pattern of how these entities try to make us even more codependent. Perhaps they themselves are so codependent to En.ki in their lofty astral realm that they believe in what they teach—I really don't know. Either way, it's a destructive path.

There is nothing wrong with helping others—we should help when and where we can—but not at the expense of ourselves. This is something I am very sure about: We can help people if they are in a jam, and we can give them information, but we can save no one, and shouldn't even try. Giving the information is all we can do. The rest is up to the other person. If they're interested, by all means, discuss it with them, show them references, and let them absorb it on their own. But never insist or force anything on anybody, or you interfere with their development/evolution, and that usually has the adverse effect from what you try to achieve. This is very important. Therefore, the best way to be Service to Others is often to leave others alone, so they can grow on their own. That's how it should be, according to the Law of Freewill.

When Sophia created us as individuated units of consciousness (separate 3-UCs), we were supposed to work together to achieve a common goal to graduate, but not at the expense of our personal evolution. Why is this so important to understand? Well, I use analogies because I like them, and it makes things easier to comprehend:

Imagine you are on an airplane. Suddenly, something is wrong, and it looks like an engine is malfunctioning. The plane is losing elevation. The flight lieutenants tell you to use the oxygen masks. But they are *very* strict with teaching us we *must* put on our own masks before we help somebody else. The reason for this is obvious—we can't help someone else if we don't help ourselves first. That's like a Golden Rule. The same thing applies to spiritual knowledge and to all other walks of life.

This is also how we heal ancestral trauma. How can we heal the past if we don't heal ourselves in the present? It is *not* selfish to put oneself first. This universe encourages it because everyone is important so each one of us can contribute to the overall expansion of the Universe. If we sacrifice ourselves for somebody else, we have failed as an individual 3-UC. Here on Earth, we have been manipulated into thinking that becoming a martyr is a good thing. It is not. It goes against universal law, so in this universe, it's detrimental. Help is fine, self-sacrifice is not. Everything else is disinformation, usually coming from channeled entities or self-proclaimed gurus. Then, of course, each situation is unique, such as helping someone who is stuck in a fire. One has to weigh one thing against another.

I presume you're leaving through the Grid this time, but let's say you weren't, and you incarnate again, after having had children. You would then reincarnate as your grandchild or great grandchild (taking the Singularity out of the equation for now). So, when you incarnate in your own seed line, what kind of life do you want? You can decide this in your current lifetime. If you heal, you heal parts of your ancestry, too, and next time you incarnate, you might have a better upbringing and a better start in life. Everybody wins. If you sacrifice yourself for others, that's the imprint you create for future generations.

The Misunderstanding of Good and Evil

Although if we choose evil, evil often will come back to us because those would be the vibrations within which we operate, there are other reasons not to choose evil.

Think of it as the Mother Goddess within us giving us both the principles of pleasure and pain. This is beneficial in the learning process because, when we developed on Tiamat, we learned to avoid pain, experiencing it as something unpleasant, and as an indicator we made a non-survival decision. Yes, it taught us lessons, but because we were freethinkers, we realized that pain is unnecessary; it's only an indicator that we needed to make other choices. In this construct, pain *is* necessary for many to advance, unfortunately. Without having experienced pain, emotional or physical, or both, in the Matrix, you would probably not be reading this now. It was likely the pain that made you ponder there is more to life than this. In the Matrix, pain grows to something different from what it was meant to be. Because of manipulation and amnesia, we attach things to those concepts, so we associate pain with evil. The Khans played on this and used it to their advantage. They used a principle the Mother Goddess embedded within us and manipulated this principle without otherwise getting their hands dirty.

The pain we suffer here is not natural. Once we experience it, we are constantly bombarded with the same pain, so we never get to learn from it. Instead, it creates a trauma-built reactive mind in a density where memory loss and reactivity are the causes of the descended Namlu'u, who was once shining in the KHAA.

Some people ask themselves why good should be preferred before evil within creation. I think the answer is not only an ethical or moral question;

it's a practical, yet existential matter. If evil would be preferred as a primary form of creation in the Universe (and maybe it is in another universe?), it does not expand the Universe because it does not expand those who inhabit it. Evil means to do harm to other beings, things, or to oneself, which makes everything lesser rather than more. That is not expansion, but degradation and destruction. If we create with good intentions and with a purpose that will benefit one's own and other's expansion, it also leads to the expansion of the Universe. It's interesting, too, that evil backwards reads as live.

Everything that keeps a being, or a soul group trapped, preventing expansion, is evil. Because this is how this construct is set up, it is essentially evil. People who try to break the cycle of reincarnation, and expand their horizons, are met by channeled entities, whose purpose is to do the exact opposite, in the disguise of being teachers and helpers. And above all, we have the Ascended Masters, who are so trapped in En.ki's net that they teach his ascension program to anyone who wants to hear. They should be called Descended Masters, because that's what they are, and what they are doing is evil. Many humans who are on their way to break free look up to these "masters," thinking they know more than they do. The only thing they know more about is the Matrix and how to manipulate.

18. The Secret Space Program

The Secret Space Program (the SSP) is a can of worms. It is a very complicated subject, and it probably deserves several standalone books if we want to dive into it in depth. There is a lot of information about this on the Internet from whistleblowers, who themselves were victims of this program, and there are books written on it, such as Peter Moon's "Montauk" series, and many others. I will only scratch the surface in this book, but I must do it because it seems to be tightly connected with the Singularity, which I will discuss in more detail in a later chapter. Everything leads toward the Singularity, which, of course, is the biggest can of worms. I have covered it in many of my writings, but there is always more to say.

Super Soldiers

To get to the other planets in the solar system, humans must also pass the physical Dome. This is something we must discuss because these Super Soldiers within the SSP claim they have been to Mars, but even to other planets in the solar system and beyond. How is that possible when we're locked inside a Dome and a Grid?

I have a lot more to learn about the SSP, but I have read case studies and testimonies of firsthand participants. From what I understand, their experiences boil down to the following:

1. It's a known fact the Super Soldiers are taken without their consent, and the ones I have listened to claim they are also MK-ULTRA victims. This means they are compartmentalized with different alters, who usually don't know about each other until these soldiers start their healing process afterwards. In MK-ULTRA mind-control, the handler, or handlers, program their victims with false memories after they have completed a mission.

2. Some Super Soldiers claim they have been outside Earth in physical bodies, some of them being space pilots, others being stationed on Mars for perhaps 25 years. Then they are put back into their original

bodies where they were hijacked, and maybe 15 minutes have passed on Earth, while 25 years passed on Mars, for example. Obviously, they did not go to Mars in their original sapiens bodies if their souls were put back into their original bodies after the mission. Some soldiers, however, claim their soul was transferred into what looked like a perfect clone of themselves, which, if this is true, would be the body they used on the mission. This could either be a "resilient body" I've discussed in different writings—a body that can better function in the harsh conditions in space. The question is, is this "cloned body" a false memory, and the body they were actually transferred to was that of a Grey? Or was it a false memory, and the person was hijacked in soul-mind-spirit only—no body involved? Or was something else happening to the person that is completely hidden behind false memories? It's hard to say.

3. Some say they were transported in "spirit" only, and they were metaphysically hijacked by military and transferred to Mars, or elsewhere.

4. This is interesting: some talk about being at a computer on another planet. This makes me think that sometimes they are not on another planet but inside a prototype to Metaverse, thinking they are off planet. To contra that, it is of course also possible they were off planet but still on a computer.

What these people have in common is that they are severely traumatized to such a degree that it's emotionally difficult to listen to their testimonies. There is no doubt in my mind that these people have experienced something, and what they are telling us is the truth, as far as they remember. However, they are also often open to the fact that what they recall can be false memories, and something happened, which is deeply buried beneath these false memories. But fact remains that these memories are extremely real to these people, and they are embedded in severe trauma.

Can Humans Enter the Solar System?

Yes, they apparently can. What I learned during the WPP years is that humans can leave the Earth, but only if they have permission from the Overlords themselves.

But how is it done? There are a few ways to do it. The person is taken and separated from their body, which is left in the bedroom, let's say. So, they travel in their astral body, which is a blueprint of their sapiens body, and at the same time, it's the Matrix avatar. Because the person is not dead, the silver cord is intact between the sapiens body and the astral body, the false soul. Therefore, one option is to let the hijacked person go through a hole in the Grid and then to Mars.

Another option would be to let the astral body travel through the fake moon, which is, from what I can tell, just a portal used in the afterlife to get to the recycling center on Mars, where the BLA is located. Interestingly, many Super Soldiers seem to have been on Mars. I would say it's more likely they transport souls through the moon portal rather than the Grid. Either way, they can bypass the Dome because they are not in physical bodies, and they go through portals. I would also suggest that the Apollo Missions and other space missions were perhaps on the moon, but not in the sense we think of it. This is just a hypothesis, but couldn't these "astronauts," also being Super Soldiers, have gone *through* the moon portal and further to Mars? Perhaps their mission was not to go to the moon in the first place, but to Mars? I remember the Pleiadians saying that the moon is artificial and was "put there" some time in the past. Let me guess... Oh, when En.ki created the BLA? The tunnel of light? The portal? Hmm...

Now we have a plausible explanation of how Super-Soldiers are transferred to Mars without their physical bodies (if that is what happens). It's very possible to do it either of these two ways, as I see it.

When it comes to transferring humans in physical bodies, it's my understanding this can't be done. We, as homo sapiens sapiens, are made to be stationary on-planet and not go out in space. If we want to go out in space in a physical sense, our consciousness must be transferred into a more resilient body, such as that of a Grey or a Reptilian, which are both cyborgs—bodies to use off planet.

How to Transfer Objects to Mars

If it's true that there is full military and Sirian activity on Mars, how do they get equipment from Earth to there? I would suggest not all equipment and objects are from Earth, but I would assume some of them are. Some equipment could be built on Mars from scratch. It's not that space rockets are fake—they probably have their valuable function. I would say they transfer equipment in the same manner the Overlords travel the Cosmic Water in hollowed-out asteroids—they use portals.

Another interesting thing is about telescopes. Until recently, the telescopes scientists had access to were placed within the atmosphere, and the result was blurry and very limited. This was because they must watch the heavens through the Dome, which works as a lens. Then they managed to (or were allowed to) transfer telescopes outside Earth, and suddenly we had much clearer pictures. We have seen many of these pictures, but what we have not seen is what else they might have discovered. Perhaps these telescopes are also capable of discovering at least some of the Dark Matter, in addition to the 4% we are used to seeing...? In juxtaposition, the pictures from the latest telescopes could be fake.

The Purpose of Super Soldiers

I believe Super Soldiers are guinea pigs and beta testers of the final Metaverse—not the version that is released by Facebook. That is just a toy so far to get people used to the idea, perhaps. The Super Soldiers are testing a much more advanced system that is now almost fully developed. These humans are being abducted and are needed to fine-tune the advanced computer system, which could very well be run from Mars, where the recycling center is, too[[64]].

As discussed earlier, it's difficult to say how much of what these soldiers recall are implanted memories and how much is true, but I am quite alarmed by the computer system a Super Soldier named Penny Bradley talked about in an interview on YouTube[[65]]. I have this eerie feeling that these Super Soldiers, who probably go back all the way to Nazi Germany, are prototypes for how the Metaverse avatars are going to operate. We know for a fact that these soldiers are compartmentalized, and each alter conforms to its task. Additionally, each person has many alters, accomplishing many things. We also know that the Overlords want us to conform when we have accessed Metaverse and the Cloud, so we can all be on the same page, which is the same page as the Overlords. If they can coordinate all humans in the Cloud to become obedient through their avatars, the Overlords only need to attach to these avatars and ride us into Orion.

How would they do this, technically speaking? It's fairly simple, now that they have studied the human psyche for so many decades by abducting some of us and made us into Super Soldiers. The Invaders have figured out exactly how to create the avatars in Metaverse. They, too, will be compartmentalized in the same fashion as the Super Soldiers—the beta testers. Thus, they do not need to mind-control all of us. They just program the avatars in the same way they have already done successfully with the Super Soldiers. Then, when humans attach to these Metaverse avatars, they also become compartmentalized and will conform. All humans will be programmed in the same way. In the beginning, Metaverse will be wonderful, and when set up correctly, people will probably love it. But then the programming starts and alters will become active in each avatar.

I don't know if this is exactly what they are planning, but if we put ourselves in the Overlords' shoes, wouldn't this be a quick way of doing it, once the ultimate Metaverse is in place?

19. Sexuality and Procreation

How Common is Sexual Procreation in the Universe?

Not that we are the *only* species in the Universe that procreates through sex, but we, and other lifeforms on Earth, may be the only species who do it as we do it. This is not how it is commonly done.

How a star race will procreate is up to the creator god, or gods, who created a certain star race in the developing worlds. They are the ones who decide what their Experiment should be all about. It seems like the Sirians also procreate similarly to us, but we are both exceptions from the rule. Most star races procreate through cloning or genetic engineering. Yes, star races who are still developing in the material worlds can die, but there is no amnesia between lives, unless the Khan Kings hijacked a star race and duplicated what they have done to us. Instead, the discarnate 2-UC gets a new body between lives, provided to them by the creator gods or the Overseers of the star system. The way I picture it is like when an avatar dies in a computer game, we take a new avatar and continue. We lose some of what we've gained in previous life, but by and large, we can just continue playing. Important to understand is that amnesia between lives exists only on Earth and on Khan occupied world, where the same, or similar, amnesia system is usually put in place.

Star Beings and Matrix Sex

There are many channeled entities, including the Pleiadians, and in addition, the Orion source, who tell us that there are many star beings who have left their home worlds but have yet to gain spiritual creativity hovering around Earth, wanting to get in here. They want to take a body here and have sex. Marduk, whose job is to guard the Grid, does his best not to let all these star beings in, but it's a monumental task sometimes, so when some star beings get in, he traps them in the reincarnation loop.

The obvious reason these star races want to experience sex is because they have heard of the pleasure it brings, but there is another, more subtle reason, too. Human women, through their orgasms, can with the right training connect with the upper regions of the KHAA, and just like the Overlords want to ride our Avatars into Orion, so do these star beings. What's different is these curious star beings don't want to conquer the KHAA and create a cosmic war—they want access to the KHAA and think they can find a shortcut into these dimensions by taking advantage of the human females. When they take a body here, it needs to be a male body. They are spiritless, so they can't take a female body and experience the KHAA because they can only have access to it through and already incarnated 3-UC woman. There are men around the planet who take advantage of women for this purpose, and they are not human. This is where much of the sexual abuse comes from. And they soon notice that the younger the girl, the purer the energy. When a child has an orgasm, its pure energy, undistorted, can be more easily directed. Thus, pedophilia.

I'm not trying to say that all pedophilia is because of star beings coming here to reach the KHAA, but it apparently happens more often than we might want to admit. The Elite use children for the same purpose, but they also use their blood and energy to rejuvenate themselves, keeping themselves young and strong. Drinking blood from a terrified child slows down the adult's aging process.

These intruding star beings don't go via the BLA, and they don't have an astral body. Therefore, it's easier for them to remember who they are, although they, too, lose their memories to some extent. But they remember their "mission" for the most part. None of them will succeed because if they're not ready for the upper regions of the KHAA, they can not take advantage of their benefits (e.g., to be spirited). Instead, when these intruders die, they will be recycled with full memory loss, like all the rest of us.

Females in ecstasy, and with their mind, can achieve extraordinary things, reaching the KHAA. Therefore, the old shamans were women, reaching for the KHAA for answers. Likewise, the prophets of old were also female, and the Ark of the Covenant was based on Mother Goddess rituals—electric energy from the ether.

Men can also reach the KHAA through orgasms, but it is more difficult, unless the male houses an equilibrium of masculine and feminine energies, which we all should strive for, because this equilibrium, this balance, is what makes us androgynous. Another way for a man to reach there is through the woman during the sex act. In a sex act, a man and a woman who want to go to the KHAA together agree to this before they have sex, and then they can start practicing.

As an interesting side note, here is something very few people know. This is information that was given to me by Orion. The Nazis used female mediums with long hair (think the Vril ladies). This was the key to the Nazis' success in World War II. They followed the Ways of the Mother Goddess, but, of course, not positively. As usual, they took advantage of something sacred and twisted it to accommodate their own purposes. What the world saw were Nazi men running Nazi Germany, but in fact, it was women who ran the show, and still probably are. The Nazi Elite had done their research and was very intelligent.

The Long Epochs of Sexuality Soon Over

Now it's time for the Overlords to stop us from procreating, and even from having sex. Because Metaverse and the Singularity will eventually lead us into the Nanoverse, sex, and procreation will become something of the past. We already know that more and more people are becoming infertile, and young men's testosterone is at an all-time low. Women are losing their sex drive, too.

In addition, all these mud-throwing debates between men and women, and transgenderism online, when taking it out of proportions, also contributes to more diversion between the sexes, and people give up—both men and women, who both feel humiliated and intimidated. There is, and has been for a long time, a chasm between men and women. But to take that debate to TikTok or elsewhere online, letting it get out of hand, and with media encouraging it, is a sure way to drop the testosterone and estrogen levels in humans and instead create a hate relationship and an increased alienation between the sexes. And as a third-party, there is the WOKE culture, stirring things up to the tenth degree. Clever, En.ki and Marduk!

None of this is a coincidence. The authorities try to tell us the drop in libido in people has mostly environmental causes, and in a way that is true. They just "forget" to tell us they are the ones who are creating the environment that makes humans lose their sex drive. For example, the toxic food, toxic environment, nanobots in the air, in food, in medicine, and in jabs; all these things, and more, contribute to the decline. Moreover, young people don't want to have children anymore because the gender nonsense has become too toxic.

In a sense, it seems like a good thing not to bring children into this world. Why support an oppressive system? Unfortunately, it's not because of that the Overlords don't want more children. It's because of the Singularity, of course. They want homo sapiens sapiens to die out and become extinct to make room for the new human, Human 4.0, where Human 1.0 were the Namlú'u, Human 2.0 were the Atlanteans, and Human 3.0 is us, homo sapiens sapiens. Human 4.0 is the cyborg human who ate from the false Tree of Life, being kept alive "forever" with technology. As mentioned before, babies will grow up in laboratories by the State—there will be no family units anymore. That being the agenda, the Overlords, obviously, don't want us to have a sex drive; it would defeat their purpose. This was all being prepared in the 1970s, when the Rockefeller family, led by David Rockefeller, started splitting the family unit by funding feminism. Feminism can be a good and just thing when not taken out of proportions; but as usual, there was an occult purpose with the movement. The new babies, raised by the State, will be the first generation of complete cyborgs. Human 4.0 children, when they grow up, will use their cosmic energy through the attached 3-UCs to power up Metaverse and keep it running.

20. The "Great aWOKEning"

The Toxic WOKE Culture

We know we live in a world that is insane, but the worst insanity right in our faces as of this writing is probably the WOKE culture. Of course, it is, as usual, run by the Elite to create division, anger, hate, boundary breaks, enforced thinking, confused children, horrendous child abuse (gender change on children), indoctrination of children, a confusion of sexes, spreading and enhancing narcissism and anti-social personality disorders (APD), preparation for the Singularity... did I forget something?

The WOKE culture is more than a hundred years old, but it started out to address racial prejudice. However, today it's a completely different beast. I am tired of stating the obvious, as if I was talking to idiots, but it's required, unless I want to have the Thought Police breathing in my neck. Here is a statement, once and for all:

> *I have nothing against homosexual people, transgenders, or any other form of genders people might prefer, and I never did. That is not the issue. People, in a freewill universe, may experience whatever they want, and sometimes that includes a change in genders. That's a person's individual right to experience, and it is none of my business.*
>
> *The problem is when this is forced upon me and the rest of the world, even using the law to make people accept a very aggressive propaganda and enforcement machine to agree to imbecile pronouns, and force transhumanism on our children. How dare you? Most transgenders think this is just as disgusting as I do—more power to them!*

What to me is astonishing is the fact that the Elite treat us regular humans as stupid one-cell organisms—now more so than ever. How dare they put such nonsense in our faces, forcing us to accept this insanity, which must be the worst insult in my life? Yes, I am upset about this because of the enforcement and the agenda behind it. And what I see in almost all these

WOKE enablers is narcissism and anti-social personality disorder (APD, i.e., psychopathy).

But if I step back and disregard my upsets, I see how this fits right into the Agenda and is a part of preparing for the Singularity, when sexes (genders) become obsolete. We, the adults, are forced to endure this nonsense, but the kids don't always have the luxury of distinguishing because their minds are not yet fully developed. They are like sponges, and when WOKE transgender people come to schools and show themselves naked to 10-year-old students to educate them that there are more than two genders, promoting transhumanism in children, the insanity is off the chart[[66]]. And when so-called "experts" suggest that all children need a sexual partner, whether it's another child or an adult, then that's the end of society. There was a twit on this recently, claiming the UN declared this, but it was fake news[[67]]. Yet, it was not entirely fake because an agenda to sexualize children is not a misnomer—there were psychologists suggesting this decades ago. Back then, they wanted to make it lawful for daddy to masturbate his daughter. After all, "daddy is the daughter's first love," was the motivation. I am not making this up. It was turned down then because the world was saner, but it will come up on the table again soon, I'm sure. Soon the world, after a little more indoctrination, might be "ripe enough" to accept such an acceptance. If the "experts" say it's good for the child, it must be true.

Long-Term Effects of Transgender Surgeries

I heard from Prof. Sam Vaknin that there are no long-term studies on the effects of a transgender operation. It is not that it hasn't been attempted, but the studies needed to stop because the subject was too sensitive, and the researchers got attacked. Of course, surgeries of this kind are nothing new, so there are people who have lived many years in the opposite gender from what they were born with. This means that there are unofficial records on long-term health effects that are not being made public. According to Vaknin, any long-term health effects from such surgeries are not entered into the patients' medical records.

It makes me wonder whether doctors tell their patients about the effects of taking lifelong hormones. Most of us know that a person who needs more testosterone or estrogen is usually warned about potential consequences, such as significantly increased cancer risks. Still, such people usually only take these hormones for a short time up to a few years. So, what will happen if a person 20 years old takes heavy-duty hormones for the rest of their life after a transgender operation? I would assume, by using logical thinking, this will increase the cancer risk exponentially.

There are some studies, however, showing a libido decrease in people who have gone through gender surgery[[68]]. This can show already after a couple of years—sometimes earlier. I have seen personal testimonies online from unhappy transgenders, crying in the videos, who wanted to explore sexuality from the perspective of whom they consider themselves to be, but the decrease in libido prevented them. Were they told this before surgery? However, there are apparently potential remedies for such a decrease, and that is more medicine. It could very well be that patients *are* informed, but their urge to go through it anyway may be stronger than the risks, creating a form of dissociation process.

The reason I bring this up is that there are interviews on the Internet with transgenders who were *not* told about serious side effects before surgery. These people, understandably, were not thrilled when these effects started to show.

Not all transgenders lose their libido, however. Some also report that their libido increases.

The Most Important Reason for the WOKE Culture

This ongoing WOKE culture, obviously, is not a grassroot movement. It started high in the echelons of power, and ultimately, it's an Overlord Agenda. As listed in the beginning of this chapter, the WOKE movement has had many consequences on society—none of them benign if you read the list. But some consequences are more important than others for the Elite.

In the 1970s, David Rockefeller funded Women's lib. to split up the family unit, and that has continued ever since.

The Rockefeller Foundation has been investing in women's empowerment since the first wave of feminism in the 1970s, when it, along with other large foundations like Carnegie and Ford, began funding women's studies programs in universities, and other efforts to research and address women's equality[[69]].

The WOKE culture removes societal values and morals on sex and genders. It's primarily directed toward the very young, who will grow up in this kind of society. Of course, the Elite and the Overlords have always targeted children when they want to introduce something new because then they can manipulate an entire generation at once, instead of trying to manipulate the adult population, which is much harder because they have experience. As Prof. Vaknin put it, *they are trying to create a chaotic society without standards* (chaos). Then order can be established on the Elite's terms, and the Singularity will be rung in as a solution to all the upheaval. To expand on that, in schools these days, the teachers are not allowed to correct bullies, so abusive kids can torture their peers without interference from adults (teachers in this case). Thus, they are defending the bullies by omission, letting other kids be traumatized and neglected. The last thing the school system wants is educated children. Dr. Jordan Peterson made case in point when he tried to implement a working school system that created interested students who increased their results with 35%[[70]]. This was not interesting to the school system, which, according to Dr. Peterson's research, is based on a system more than a hundred years old, which purpose was to create obedient soldiers and workers who were clever enough to follow a scheduled routine in a work environment. Since then, nothing has changed.

The WOKE movement helps to desexualize society, forcing this movement on kids, so they grow up with a distorted view of sex, genders, and pronouns. They may no longer call their peer "he" or "she," but must ask their classmates what pronouns they prefer today because it might not be the same as yesterday. This has now become a mandatory rule in many schools, and if the students do not abide to this, they are punished and can lead to expulsion. You are not allowed to call someone "he" or "she." But the worst thing is that many parents accept this as something potentially good. What has the world come to? All individual thinking is thrown out the window. It is shown in IQ studies that the average IQ in the general population has decreased substantially over the last couple of decades.

They are degrading us humans, and it's happening quickly now. Pushing and promoting transgenderism on children is the most vicious thing on their public agenda right now.

21. The Singularity and Human 4.0

All Humans are Already Cyborgs

For a few decades now, we in the alternative community have discussed a future where the Elite plan to put our consciousness in cyborg bodies, i.e., bodies that are partly biological and partly machine, made with nanotechnology. This agenda upset people because many humans want to remain biological beings. However, that is not the actual issue, believe it or not.

Bluntly speaking, we already are cyborgs, and we have been cyborgs since homo sapiens sapiens were created in the beginning of the Matrix, nearly 10,000 years ago. Our physical bodies, genetically modified by En.ki and Isis (aka NIN.MA), later involving Marduk and Ereškigal, are biotechnological machines. This means we are already A.I. to a significant degree. Our bodies are programmed to accomplish certain automatic tasks, such as breathing, regulating heartbeats, and to self-heal. This, and so much more, is something the body can do without the direct and sentient involvement of our consciousness. The body just needs the battery necessary to trigger these functions, and the battery is the consciousness we invest in this half-machine we call our body. As a part of our sapiens body package also comes an artificial soul and mind, as discussed in a previous chapter.

Thus, the issue is not whether they will force us into a new cyborg; it's about *why* this is being done. People who want to stay in the Matrix welcome the fact that nanotechnology will extend their physical lives, potentially for a very long time. Some would call it "forever," although this is an elusive word. In fact, "forever" in this case is just a short period, since the Overlords are planning to invade Orion. The new cyborg bodies, which we may coin Human 4.0, will only last as long as it takes for the Invaders to conquer Orion, taking into consideration that they would succeed, of course. But even if they won't succeed and will be defeated, Orion will terminate the 4.0 bodies anyway because when humans trapped in Metaverse are free to leave the Matrix, the Human 4.0 bodies become obsolete.

Human 4.0, the bodies built with nanotechnology, will function as batteries, keeping Metaverse running. Astral bodies, as we know them, together with the BLA, will be obsolete, and the 3-UC will instead be trapped directly inside a Metaverse avatar, which will be the new artificial soul, mind, and body, stuck within a Fourth Construct, inside a new Grid, encompassing the infamous Cloud, where all Metaverse consciousness will be assembled.

Metaverse and the Singularity—Why Now?

Why has En.ki waited so long to lure us into Metaverse? Why not at the beginning of the Matrix?

There are several reasons for this. The obvious reason is he needed to create homo sapiens sapiens first, so the human soul group could go through evolution again, after having suffered complete amnesia in the early Matrix. Another reason goes hand in hand with that: The Overlords must manipulate us to such a degree that we enter the Nanoverse willingly and with consent. We must have adjusted to the Overlords' mindset and copied it. It took them almost 10,000 years to do so. Now, humankind is close to being ripe enough to be lured in, but perhaps not ripe enough. From what I've learned, the Overlords are desperate to get the Metaverse up and running because of the Ultimatum. Yes, the Overlords want war, but on *their* terms. They want to avoid extended war in the Earth's vicinity because they feel vulnerable here. They would not win if Orion set in their forces, and they know that. Their only chance is to ride our Avatars.

Why then does Orion not attack them now instead of waiting? Again, it's because of many things, such as keeping humankind as hostages. But there is another reason that has not been discussed as much, so let's discuss it now.

Patents and Genetic Tinkering of our DNA

The human scientific community has betrayed their own species in a much more severe manner than previously thought, often unbeknownst to them. We all know that they have received technology from the gods, so they can genetically manipulate and tinker with our DNA and mRNA. The vaccines are a typical example of this, but there is, of course, the entire nanotechnological aspect of remodeling us into Human 4.0. But here is the big issue:

The Overlords have manipulated the science community to take patents on genetic tinkering. Our patent laws work in such a way that because these patents have been approved, the Overlords now consider themselves owning the new species, 4.0. The new human becomes the Overlords' property. But if humans patent the tinkering, how can the Overlords, in extension, own us? It's because we were already hybridized when they created different seed lines long ago (see Chapter 1). This is illegal from a cosmic perspective, so the Overlords need to justify that—particularly now when they might get caught and put to trial. Thus, by patenting tinkering of DNA, we humans approve of genetic manipulation, and because the Overlords are the ones doing it, it now becomes legal, since we give our consent.

The Overlords can then claim us as theirs without breaking universal laws. Because this is an agreement between the Khan Kings and the science community, it's legally binding, so if Orion interferes, they break human laws and commit a crime against the human legal system. There are so many patents that are approved behind our backs, but because a patent is a legal thing, it's not allowed, legally, to break it. Therefore, this is another reason why the Queen's forces can't just come.

Contradictory: Population Control vs. Increase

Most of us have heard of the Georgia Guidestones and population control. They want to reduce the population significantly. How come then that the population has been increasing "out of control" over the last few decades? Why wasn't this population increase stopped in its cradle by the Overlords? I have seen no satisfactory explanations for this and how it's going to be done, so let's see if we still can solve that riddle.

I have learned that out of the 7-8 billion people on the planet, the Overlords most likely only need about 3%, which is approximately 192 million people, for their purpose of invading Orion. Still, that is quite an army. Therefore, if over 192 million people will join Metaverse, there are only so many 3-UCs the Overlords can handle. After all, the gods are much fewer in numbers than the human soul group, and each Overlord needs to ride an Avatar. The rest will be cannon fodder, possibly sent to the frontline to protect the possessed humans farther back in the lineup. So, there is a boundary for how many people they need. The rest they don't care for. They also don't want too many non-possessed humans to take part in the Final Battle because it can easily get out of control and work in Orion's favor.

Then why 7-8 billion people? The answer is simple once we hear it: They needed this vast number of humans to gather information to feed the Metaverse. The Internet, including desktops, laptops, smartphones, iPads, iPods, nano-botted humans, and satellites, etc., have all contributed to assembling information on us all to capture our consciousness once we're dedicated to Metaverse. It is my understanding that this is now almost accomplished, and now it's time for population reduction. So, how is that going to be done?

In the past, world wars took care of it temporarily, so the population did not increase too fast, but soon enough, after these major wars, the human soul group continued to reproduce quickly. Therefore, wars don't take care of it either, obviously. Wars still fill a function in population culling, but something more drastic needs to be done. Thus came the pandemic. Of course, the entire event was planned and manipulated, and the secret government completely overloaded us with lies and gaslighting. But this event was not meant to kill off the population—it was only a precursor for something else: the vaccines. First, we must be scared to death of a global threat that, according to the false narrative, could potentially kill off most of the population, and there was no way to stop it unless the ingenious scientists came up with vaccines (which they did in record-speed. No time to waste—the Agenda must move forward). In the vaccines, they could put whatever they needed to include, such as nanotechnology, DNA mutation technology, and other additives that could target particular individuals with certain types of DNA. These are the ones, I suggest, who later got sick and died from the shots, and still do. The Elite wants it to take some time between the shot and the death moment, so no obvious connection can be made between shot and death. This is also what we're seeing. Other people seem to have very few side effects from the poison. This doesn't mean they're the lucky ones. They are just the ones minutely selected by the Overlords to be physically prepared for Metaverse. There are apparently certain DNA combinations, or something else, that's not compatible with what is needed to enter Metaverse. This will not kill off enough people, however, and it's not meant to. They still need people of current generations to enter Metaverse. The adjustment of numbers of people they want will be accomplished later, as I will explain in a minute.

Another thing related to vaccines is infertility and decreased libido in both young and old people. They want us to stop procreating, and they are quite successful. On top of that, we have social media that increases narcissism and creates personality modifications. The WOKE culture also helps the Agenda in this sense: It confuses our children about human anatomy, and the generation growing up now will, besides having to take vaccines, etc., be reluctant to have sex and start families. Soon, every child will be brain implanted to be fully compatible with Metaverse, and via this implant, and connected to Elon Musk's satellites, all humans can be remotely manipulated, and their hormones tampered with—no more sexual desire, or desire to build families. After that, we have the laboratories, where they use stem cells to create new life, i.e., new artificial humans, who will be perfectly equipped for Metaverse. These will be the cyborgs we have been discussing for so many years—the *true* cyborgs because they will be cyborgs from birth—Human 4.0. I would argue that through the laboratories, the Elite will determine the number of people they want on the planet. As the older generations die off, the scientists can create new bodies that won't die, and they will make sure they have about 192 million bodies to experiment with, just as planned. The rest of the population will soon be dead and gone anyway.

So, what happens with the excess 3-UCs whom they don't need in Metaverse and the Singularity? Well, they will not be recycled, so perhaps they will be kept locked up somewhere in the astral, but I don't know. This does not pertain to those who will exit through the Grid but will pertain to those who won't. Some will be glued to the laboratory babies until the quota is filled, and the fate of others is unknown. Perhaps they get eaten, or their used astral body energy will feed Metaverse.

Thus, humankind, or as many of us as they need, will be connected to the Cloud, which is technologically run by a Supercomputer, which I was talking about in the Singularity book in 2016[[71]]. There, everybody will be plugged into a hive-mind. Our thoughts will be interconnected, so the more decent and compassionate people must mingle with the minds of murderers, rapists, and serial killers. I don't even want to imagine how that would be like.

The Global Traumatization of the Human Soul Group

No one can deny that we live in unprecedented times because, due to the Internet and global network broadcasting, the Elite can traumatize an entire world at once, which they also are doing. Without too much effort, they can make something up, or twisting true information, present it as fact, and shovel it upon us, creating immense fear and anxiety in people. We may argue this is because they want to control us, and that is true. Another reason is that they feed from our emotions, and by instigating fear and terror, they get a lot of loosh. That is also true. However, there is another reason, too.

By traumatizing us on a global scale, we all develop the same fears and trauma, which is automatically added to the unconscious mind (the common mind of the human soul group that we all share). Thus, they can trigger us globally, and most of us will react the same, which creates a uniform vibration the Overlords need to attach to us in Metaverse. They are not coming to us to possess us for the purpose of the Orion Invasion; *we will come to them!*

They reside in the lower dimensions of the astral, which the Pleiadians refer to as the Machine Kingdom. There, everything is technology. That's where they want us, mentally. Then we are within the same frequency range as the Overlords. From there, it's a piece of cake to take us over because we vibrate within their normal frequency range and we have become like them (something that is happening more rapidly now). Look around you: Are we living in a more spiritual environment than 20-30 years ago? Or are we living in a robotic, super-technological environment, where human feelings and emotions are frowned upon, and we are gaslit into showing less love, compassion, and empathy? I think the answer is obvious: *We are approaching the Overlords' Machine Kingdom as a soul group.*

Merging with our Ancestors

We have discussed hive-mind, pertaining to the Singularity. I was also told that if we enter Metaverse and get trapped in the Cloud, we will merge with all our ancestors on our genetic line, without having any control over it. This means, all these people in a person's ancestral line, some of them perhaps being murderers and rapists, will now be ONE with this person. Horrible thought. Why do the Overlords do this? Because this mimics who *they* are, and they want us to be like them, so they can easily control us.

All this, I believe, are ideas shared between En.ki and Marduk, but these two gods[[72]] are still not on the same page. As a reminder from what we discussed in Chapter 8, Marduk wants to get his hands on Metaverse and the Singularity and take En.ki out of the equation. En.ki, from his position, wants to do the same with Marduk. Two people in control of Metaverse are one too many. Who wins the race is for us irrelevant—the outcome will still be the same for us, although a bit harsher if Marduk gets the upper hand.

The Nanoverse and Quantum Mechanics

Dr. Marco Sacchi, the project lead, and Royal Society University Research Fellow at the University of Surrey, said:

> "Many have long suspected that the quantum world – which is weird, counter-intuitive and wonderful – plays a role in life as we know it. While the idea that something can be present in two places at the same time might be absurd to many of us, this happens all the time in the quantum world, and our study confirms that quantum tunnelling also happens in DNA at room temperature[[73]]."

When we discuss Orion, what we are talking about the quantum and sub-quantum worlds (which *is* Orion). Therefore, in the Matrix, we are connected and influenced by the quantum world; that's our home. That's where our DNA originates—En.ki just manipulated it to restrict our senses to this particular Matrix System.

Now. when scientists have gotten the hang of quantum mechanics (which makes it possible to manipulate the quantum world—the nano world, or the Nanoverse/Orion), they can also manipulate us and the Matrix at large much easier. To explore the Nanoverse, top scientists, today and in the past, got help from the Overlords, who "channel" information into selected humans with brilliant minds (such as Tesla and others) as a part of the plan. From there, they can easily manipulate our DNA in laboratories. In the beginning of the Third Construct (the Matrix), the Overlords could do it themselves because they still had creative abilities, but now they need us to do it for them. Therefore, the only reason why scientists were made aware of the quantum world was so they can transmute humankind, using nanotechnology to make the transition into the Nanoverse via Metaverse.

Also, regarding how something can be present in several places simultaneously, we have many times discussed how an Avatar can split itself to exist simultaneously in several locations in the Universe and across the dimensions. We just split our spirit-fires. Quantum physicists at high levels know this, but they are not revealing that part to the public.

Louie Slocombe, a PhD student at the Leverhulme Quantum Biology Doctoral Training Centre and co-author of the study, said:

> "There is still a long and exciting road ahead of us to understand how biological processes work on the subatomic level, but our study – and countless others over the recent years – have confirmed quantum mechanics are at play. In the future, we are hoping to investigate how tautomers produced by quantum tunnelling can propagate and generate genetic mutations[[74]]."

Here, they just revealed something they already know the answer to and are implementing big time to prepare for the Singularity; but they are pretending they are still researching it. They know *much* more than they are telling us, and they are using these technologies on us as we speak. In fact, the technology they are hiding from us is many decades ahead of what has been released and implemented so far. Still, I am being modest here because most likely technology is *much* further ahead than just a few decades.

The SWS—the Supercomputer in Indiana

SWS stands for "Sentient World Simulation," and it refers to a supercomputer in Indiana, USA. What this computer does is uncanny, to say the least: *It creates a synthetic parallel world with our avatars and is collecting data on us.*

> Sentient World Simulation is the name given to the current vision of making SEAS a "continuously running, continually updated mirror model of the real world that can be used to predict and evaluate future events and courses of action.
>
> [...]
>
> The Sentient World Simulation project (SWS) is to be based on SEAS. The ultimate goal envisioned by Alok R. Chaturvedi on March 10, 2006 was for SWS to be a 'continuously running, continually updated mirror model of the real world that can be used to predict and evaluate future events and courses of action. SWS will react to actual events that occur anywhere in the world and incorporate newly sensed data from the real world. [...] As the models influence each other and the shared synthetic environment, behaviors and trends emerge in the synthetic world as they do in the real world. Analysis can be performed on the trends in the synthetic world to validate alternate worldviews. [...] Information can be easily displayed and readily transitioned from one focus to another using detailed modeling, such as engineering level modeling, to aggregated strategic, theater, or campaign-level modeling.'[[75]]."

Imagine what they can do with this technology, and then imagine how it *is* used today in preparation for Metaverse, and the event-control of the future virtual reality simulation[[76]].

A powerful 'sentient' computer simulation of billions of people and nations that 'mirrors' reality is up-and-running and likely tracking your every move[[77]].

It is obvious to me that this is what the Department of Defense is using this program for as its main function. The official version of how it's used to predict what enemy nations' strategic plans in the future is just a secondary function.

Here is more, solidifying what we have discussed for many years, now turning into reality:

> "Even so, many may find it equally disturbing that each avatar in the SWS virtual reality universe does represent a thorough activity profile of who you are and what you are doing in the real world.
>
> [...]
>
> Every time you engage with cyberspace, the SWS vacuums up that data point and adds it to the profile of your avatar.
>
> [...]
>
> This creates a "predictive model" of you and tells SWS operators how you are likely to react in certain situations as well as how you will perform or act in a group dynamic situation.
>
> [...]
>
> ... it collects a wide range of data points that essentially provides a complete profile of every person, including what they do, what they like, how they act in certain situations, and so on[[78]]."

It now becomes clear what this is all about, doesn't it? And there are reactions against this, even within academia. Here is something that very much corresponds with what I have communicated over the years:

"This not only invades our privacy but can also cause severe damage to society. Knowing that there is a copy of each of us in the virtual world, which can think and behave like us, and whose actions can be predicted by the authorities is a far more intimidating invasion. This will have a negative impact on societies by reducing trust between citizens and government, as well as among people — altering normal human behavior since the populace will be conscious of the fact that there is a copy of them in a virtual world without their consent[79]."

So, this is another piece of the puzzle, explaining how they transfer our consciousness into Metaverse, mirroring everything we do online. I hope it's getting clearer now how they do this from a more technological and scientific standpoint. There is no doubt about it, is it? By mirroring us, being able to predict our actions and reactions, they can completely control us when we enter Metaverse. The rest is a breeze—the Overlords just need to connect to the ultimate mind-controlled hive-mind. Once we're in Metaverse, the time from when the Metaverse grabs us and has us in its claws to when the Invasion of Orion will happen will be brief. Everything is already prepared.

The Pleiadians often said that the problem the Overlords have with us humans is that we are unpredictable, and therefore, difficult to control. This seems to have been eliminated now. In Metaverse, we will instead be perhaps 98% predictable (made-up number), and that's enough for the Overlords to control us all as the hive-mind we will become.

Can you Spot a Deepfake From a Real Person?

We obviously need to get used to new terms, as those appear very frequently these days. One such term is "deepfake." What does it mean? Deepfake denotes artificial intelligence technology being used to manipulate videos and audio in a way that replicates real life.

This means that now everyone, with a little practice, can make a YouTube video of you, for example, with an avatar so much resembling you that it will fool the viewer, thinking it's the real you. Then, the YouTube creator can imitate your voice that it sounds just like you (considering he has a sample of your voice). Lastly, he can put words in your mouth you have never uttered and would never dream of uttering. Thus, running smear campaigns on people we don't like is now going to be a simple task, and it can ruin people's careers, destroy relationships, and so much more. People will never know whether you said these things or not. It's your word against the YouTube video. This only shows how easily this technology can be misused and abused, putting innocent people in dangerous situations.

How can anyone think this will not happen? It's already happened. Do people think there will be some kind of working regulation against this? Good luck with that!

What about Google? Silicon Valley? Are they all evil crooks trying to destroy humankind? To be honest, no! Believe it or not, but most people working for Google, for example, are enthusiastic good but naïve people, thinking AI technology will enhance our lives in the near future, including giving us eternal life. Someone interviewed the CEO of Google, Sundar Pichai, and asked him if he didn't think it was dangerous to let AI loose, since some androids have threatened to exterminate humans in the future. Mr. Pichai answered he was aware of this, and it greatly bothers him to the point where he is very anxious about the whole thing. When asked why he doesn't call it quits, he replied that it's gone too far. It's unstoppable. Even if he would shut down the entire AI project, some brilliant teenager somewhere would still be able to go in and complete the work, and with "work," it implies using AI technology viciously. So, there is no way back, the CEO said. Well, even if that is true, it does not, in my opinion, justify Mr. Pichai to continue. If I were him, I would do the only decent thing—quit my job when I noticed things got overboard and go out and warn people against the process.

Moreover, for some time, I have spoken about AI taking over art, entertainment, music, visual art, and literature. Now it's happening. We might think AI art can't compete with art created by a human creator because human creators have feelings and emotions. AI doesn't.

If so, I have news.

We don't need to think farther than to the psychopaths in our lives. They are evidently without genuine emotions and feelings, but they can very successfully imitate our deepest emotions because they have studied them all their lives, and they think their own survival depends on being able to duplicate genuine emotions. Often, they do it better than the genuine person. The difference, however, lies in the word *genuine*. If an emotionless human can mimic emotions that well, why can't AI? It can, and it already does. For example, if I write a novel, it might take a year from start to finish. If I were to tell an AI my plot ideas, AI can write the book in twenty seconds. Dr. Jordan Peterson did an experiment with this, and he said he was shocked because he could not distinguish between his own writing and that of AI. This means, in the future, all we need to do is to give AI an idea, and AI can write an entire book in a matter of no time on a computer fast enough to write that fast. This takes away the human creative abilities from us here in the Matrix.

Did the First Singularity Happen in Atlantis?

The end period of Atlantis, i.e., the Second Construct before the Matrix, is known to have been highly technologically developed. Remnants of these cultures still exist—both under the ocean, where ruins of old, magnificent cities, have been discovered, and in Antarctica, where impressive remnants of these ancient, advanced civilizations have been detected.

We also know that Noah's Flood happened because of En.ki's tinkering with human genetics. And the gods, already then, raped human women, or seduced them, creating hybrid offspring, which is a high crime in the Universe, and that alone renders the Experiment void, and it needs to be terminated. It's almost like if you try to isolate something in a laboratory, and you forget to put on your sterile gloves, so germs get into the experiment. That makes the experiment corrupted and void, and it must be terminated.

Already in the 1990s, Marciniak's Pleiadians said that Atlantis was more technologically advanced than our present society. Space travel was common. I would go so far as to say that En.ki, behind everybody's back, created the first Singularity already then, perhaps 11,000 years ago, just before the Deluge.

I would further argue that En.ki's Singularity was hijacked by Marduk, who took over and manipulated a group of humans to invade the Pleiades, where En.ki at that time had a stronghold. I think it happened like this: En.ki created the first Singularity, and when he was good to go, he was detected, and the entire Experiment was terminated by Orion in a Flood. En.ki fled to the Pleiades, where he had a stronghold to which he could escape the wrath of his brother, En.lil, and the rest of the Orion crew. However, Marduk then saw his opportunity to use the hijacked human group against En.ki, so he manipulated that group to invade the Pleiades and take it over, having their Avatars possessed by Khan Kings, forcing these humans to invade and take the star systems. I think the invasion of the Pleiades that the Pleiadians talk about was not a human idea—it came from Marduk. And this time around, Marduk is trying to do something similar, with the exception that this time he goes for Orion directly, using En.ki's plan to do this.

I also suspect the first Singularity did not play out in a Metaverse, but in the current physical world. En.ki put humans into Grey cyborgs, which is backed up by channeled material, where the channeling entities claim to be us in the future on a different timeline. Almost all of them claim to be "Greys.". En.ki might not yet have mastered nanotechnology enough at that time to create a functioning Metaverse. Putting humans in Grey "space suit" could have been a pilot project Marduk then sneaked up on and took over when En.ki looked the other way. Thus, the invasion of the Pleiades happened in the physical realm. Because of the resilience of the Grey body type, humans could be sent as an army through wormholes and stargates to enter the Pleiades.

So, who is most likely to win the current race, Marduk or En.ki? It's hard to say, but we might get further hints by studying world politics continuously. Who is gaining ground? Marduk's or En.ki's team?

How can we take Advantage of the Overlords' Agenda?

A few people have asked me what to do if you're young and will be alive and well when the Singularity is in place, and you refuse to participate? I think there might be a way around it. But how?

When the Metaverse participants have been engulfed by the Cloud, the Grid will most likely come down. And even if it does not come down completely, it's going to be so damaged that we are no longer talking about holes like in a Swiss cheese—we're talking about a Grid that's hanging on loose threads, like a damaged spiderweb that's been cut through many times. Survivors here on Earth, not being stuck in the new Grid (the Cloud), will become more multidimensional because there is a huge pathway to the KHAA where the Grid used to be. Also, there will be survivors here on Earth who know about the Grid and Orion. They will certainly educate others, and when these young people eventually die off from old age or disease, they can easily leave the Matrix. The road to freedom is wide open. The trick for those alive when Metaverse is fully functional is to refuse to participate. Therefore, it will most likely be necessary to build groups or tribes to survive on what nature can bring. *Back to Nature*, so to speak. I don't think the Overlords, or the Elite, will tamper too much with these survivors. They have more important things to concentrate on. I am quite confident they will leave these groups alone.

22. More on the Grid and Death

As the Orion source once told me back in 2012, "The Grid keeps the energy trapped [and] the tunnel/machine is what recycles the souls."

With this in mind, the following is a direct quote from Barbara Marciniak, channeling the Pleiadians:

"A frequency fence, something like an electrical fence, was put around the planet to control how much the frequencies of humans could be modulated and changed.

As the story goes, this frequency fence made it very difficult for the frequencies of light—information—to penetrate. When light frequencies were able to penetrate the control fence, there was no light to receive them. The humans' DNA was unplugged, the light-encoded filaments were no longer organized, so the creative cosmic rays that brought light did not have anything to plug into and hold onto." -*"Bringers of the Dawn, Teachings of the Pleiadians", 1992*[[80]].

As you can see, the Grid was mentioned before I got in touch with the Orion source in 2010. I should also note that the Pleiadians and the Orion source did not know about each other. There is also another reference from Marciniak's Pleiadians, which is not in the book "Bringers of the Dawn," where they say there were a few isolated holes in the Grid, at least as far back as the 1980s, which makes sense because the Orion source entered around that time through a hole in the Grid.

The Orion-Khan King Battle of 2008-2009

The Grid was also severely damaged in 2008-2009, when there was a space battle between Orion and the Khan Kings in the solar system. Orion did not enter with the purpose of raging war or fighting a battle; but the Khan Kings, who saw them coming, defended "their" territory, and a battle emerged. The reason the Orions came was to shoot holes in the Grid to make it easier for us humans to wake up. The mission was a success, and then the Orion troops withdrew. It showed that the damage was so severe that the Overlords can not repair it up to this day, and as the Orion source said, *soon they need to take it down*. And they will. If not any sooner, at least by the time the Singularity is in place.

One consequence of the Grid damage was that the Overlords since then have had a harder time recycling souls because the Grid is "playing up," as the Orion source put it. Exactly what "playing up" means in technical terms, I don't know.

Retrieving our Memories after Exiting the Grid

I have had many discussions about this on different platforms, and I've written about it, but I want to emphasize the following because if I am to trust the most important source I have had, being not-from-here, we do *not* need to worry about retrieving our spirit fires from the Matrix after we have exited. People have been concerned that if we leave spirit fires behind, connected to other lifetimes on Earth, we don't fully exit, and we need that spirit fire back. If not for any other reason, we need it to regain our full memories from our time in the Matrix.

I have now learned that this is not a concern. Once you exit, you will reunite with your spirit body, and all the energy you invested in the Matrix will be retrieved, as well. If your name is Mary, for example, and you exit through the Grid, you exit as Mary, even though you have had other lifetime experiences on Earth, too. Those lifetime experiences pertain to your ancestral line because you reincarnate into the same ancestral line lifetime after lifetime. However, in the BLA, before you are shot down into a new body in your ancestral line, you are memory wiped, and you incarnate with a blank slate. The only memories, if ever so vague, that you have are those of your ancestors, and those include previous incarnations of *you*, as your own great-grand parent, for example, and before that, their great-grand parent, and so on, in a direct line way back in "time." You have no soul memories because they are completely wiped out between lives. It's important to understand that your memories are not collected in your soul fires, but in the Matrix avatar, which is being destroyed and split into pieces in the BLA.

Despite the memory wipe between lives (and this is important), you, as Mary, living your life in the 21st century, still have all your complete memories buried in your DNA. A tiny part of it you may experience as "flashbacks," and short sequences of past lives, which are not always yours, but could be the memories/experiences of someone else in your ancestral line. Therefore, past lives regression therapy is only partially helpful because you might very well tune into your ancestor's life, which was not your own life.

It is because of this Orion is so concerned with whom you are in *this* lifetime because that is the accumulated personality you've gained from a long line of ancestry assembled into one lifetime—your current one. Some people have asked me, "If someone is a murderer in *this* life, why can't they come to Orion? After all, the same soul might have been saintlike in another life..." Although this may or may not be the case, it's irrelevant. Even if Mary was saintlike in a certain lifetime, that obviously did not transfer over to Mary in her present life as a killer. And it is Mary, the murderer, who will exit through the Grid because that's what she has become over the millennia. That's her "soul evolution." Because of the accumulation of experiences on her ancestral line, she ended up as a murderer, and that's what she is now. Therefore, Orion does not want to let her loose in Orion.

So, when we retrieve the consciousness, we, as spirit bodies "outside" the Matrix, have invested in this simulation, we retrieve the memories of our *entire* ancestral line, which is the accumulation of our experiences in the Matrix. This can be done because DNA is not restricted to the Matrix, but extends into the KHAA and to our spirit bodies. Therefore, please don't worry about what, or what not, to retrieve in energy. And if there is anything we need help with after we have exited, I was promised we will get help with that. Just concentrate on being who you are in the present and do your best to improve—the rest will follow.

Once we reconnect with our true spirit body, we will merge our soul experiences with it, and it will be added to our memories and experiences. Because we also had an existence before the Matrix, those memories and experiences are already collected in the spirit body and our true Avatar (not the artificial soul/astral body, which we will shed on our way out). So, our old experiences before the Matrix, besides the Matrix experiences, will thus become our overall experience, which will make up our ultimate personality.

People often talk about Oversouls, but the Oversoul is the "Overspirit," i.e., our spirit body—the ultimate "person." That is how we were created. We were made as a Three Unit Composite (3-UC), comprising soul, mind, and spirit body, and each of us is our own 3-UC. This was meant to be the whole of us—no extra "Oversoul" or "Overspirit." The 3-UC should become her own Overspirit by accumulating experiences. It's true that the Queen could be considered our ultimate Overspirit, but apparently, she does not see it that way because she will not interfere with our development or act as a superior source of experience. We are our own Higher Selves, which, in my opinion, is how it should be. This makes each of us independent and separated from our Cosmic Mother as individuals, just like toddlers separate from their mothers (if the mother is not a narcissist).

On Exiting Through the Grid

Do you feel powerful? Ready to challenge the Overlords? Feeling so mighty that you think you can accomplish anything you want in Orion?

If so, congratulations! But most of us probably do *not* feel that powerful. Most of us instead have many doubts about ourselves and our abilities, both here in the Matrix and when we enter Orion. This is normal under the circumstances. We tend to think all other beings must be more powerful than us because we have been so invalidated, traumatized, and gaslit here on Earth through the millennia. We are afraid of so many things, big and small, and not the least to exit through the Grid. To us, that is unfamiliar territory.

However, we must not forget who we *really* are, i.e., immortal, powerful, creative beings of a kind that have never been created before. We have nothing to fear. Beings, both in the astral and in Orion, know who we are, and if we set our intention to exit despite the fear we might still hold in the exit moment, not letting that fear get the best of us, no one is going to stop us because they simply can't. The only way to stop a determined being is if that same being compromises with his or her intention because of inner fear or from a distraction outside. Other than that, no one can stop that person. *Once you're out, you will know your* true *power!*

Is the Grid the Only Way Out of the Matrix?

For those who want to exit as soon as possible, I have seen no good or working alternatives to the Grid. And to be honest, why do we want an alternative in the first place? Can there really be an easier way to exit than through a hole in the Grid? Even if there were other ways out, would they really be simpler than going through the Grid? I would like to see that soulution. Despite the amazing opportunity we have regarding the Grid exit, people still ask me about alternative routes, something I think is unnecessary. However, I can see where they might come from; maybe they want a Plan B in case Plan A fails. That is understandable.

There seem to be other ways to leave the Matrix, but they are not as immediate as the Grid, which is still the alternative that is closest in time (after body death), and the easiest route to follow. We do not want to reincarnate again, obviously, but as I mentioned before, those who resist Metaverse and the Singularity can live out their lives as renegades, and then leave the Matrix without the Grid, which at that point will probably have been taken down. Therefore, the way out of the Matrix and to Orion will lie wide open.

Also, in Chapter 25, "Redemption," I will mention another option, but it is more uncertain, depending on how far the Overlords can go with their Agenda. Reviewing some more of my discussions with the Orion source, it looks like Orion is more confident than I thought that the Overlords will fail their Orion Invasion.

I have also encountered other soulutions from people out there on how to leave the Matrix, but with the information I have, nothing of it has convinced me.

How the Grid Might Look Like Today

A good friend of mine, who is also an excellent remote viewer, said to me he has seen the Grid, and how it looks like in present time. I want to include it here with an explanation for the reader's consideration because his observations coincide with mine. Here is a picture of the current Grid, very close to how he saw it:

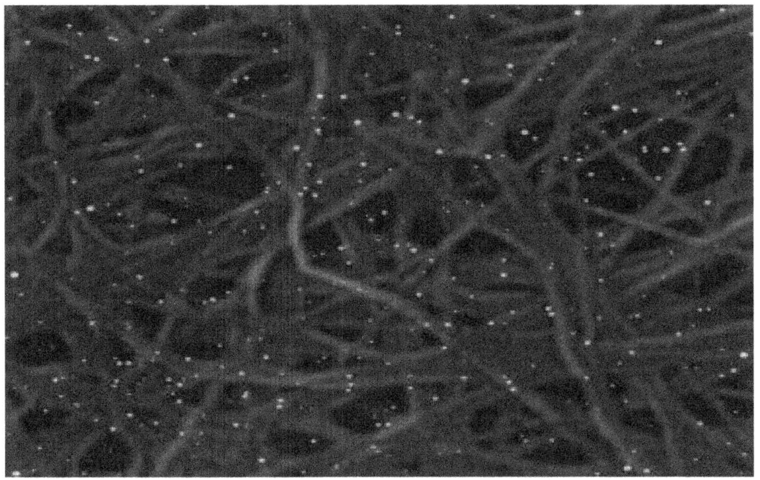

Image 22:1. The potential current version of the Grid.

The following is his commentary on the above picture:

"Here is what I saw when I looked up at the sky one night in 2021. It was in Salt Lake City, Utah. I used photo editing software to make a composite that's a fair representation. It's not 100%, but the picture gives you a good idea. Whatever happened to the Grid resulted in a lot of damage and now there are many 'holes'.

[...]

The black areas [in the image] are the 'holes.' The dim white fiber-looking areas are the Grid.

My experience seeing the Grid was in the evening, awake, and not remote viewing.

I did not remote view the process of going through the Grid, so I did not remote view it as a target. My target was on the outside of the Grid and the time was in the past.

Linear time does not exist to the mind outside the Grid like we experience within the Patrix[[81]]. Once outside, all time exists in a present.

It's hard to describe, but imagine being in a library full of books. They are all present, but you don't experience the stories within a book until you set your mind to open and read the words on the page in sequence. The sentences build an experience. Another way one might look at it is a flip book of an animated character. The book exists in the present, but you don't experience the moving character until you flip through the pages. Each page exists in the present, but you 'perceive' a character moving if you flip the pages[[82]]."

I think this brilliantly explains the Grid and what we can experience, in relation to time, right after we have exited. I should add that the white spots in *Image 22:1* are stars outside the Matrix, still seen through the filter of a human body.

In the light of the information we have, I think this image and the explanation given summarize well the condition of the Grid today. As the reader can see, the holes are no longer like those in a Swiss cheese. These holes are huge, and no one should have any problem penetrating the Grid.

23. The Gnostics and the Jesus Story

The Jesus Myth

Perhaps the most successful deception the Overlords have pulled off is the deception of the Biblical and Gnostic Jesus Christ (Yeshua). By this, I don't mean there is nothing to the Jesus myth, but the truth is far from what we have been told. This will also be obvious to the readers who have read the Wes Penre Papers and The ORION Book, volume 1, and pondered enough over it. The Universe is feminine; the Creatrix is feminine, and a civilization who is on task knows that the true Divine is feminine, not masculine. How come, then, that both Jesus and God are masculine in the New Testament and in the Nag Hammadi Gnostic texts? That goes against the entire concept of Sophia being the Creatrix. If she'd have arranged for a descended Jesus as a savior (which she never would do), this Jesus would come in a feminine form, and her Mother would be Sophia. Therefore, the entire Jesus myth is based on a patriarchal cosmic view. It is true that in the Nag Hammadi, many gospels convey we are our own saviors, but that does not take away from the fact that they address a masculine God (En.ki) and his masculine son (Marduk). In the Nag Hammadi, Khan En.lil is added as a Divine masculine force, when he is a former Sirian-Arcturian Khan King, who has repented and joined forces with Orion. Therefore, if a Divine message would be conveyed to us, it would come from the Mother Goddess, not Khan En.lil, aka Jesus Christ in the Nag Hammadi, where Sabaoth is Jesus in the flesh, funneling Khan En.lil's Divine message.

Another objection to the validity of the New Testament and the Nag Hammadi texts is the unlikeliness that Prince En.lil, aka Prince Ninurta, aka Archangel Michael, would incarnate in the bloodline of David, and ultimately Noah. This is En.ki's bloodline. It makes little sense. And Marduk thereby stole the title of Archangel Michael, which will be important to remember later in this chapter. After having seen through this fraud, I am also questioning the identity of Sabaoth in the Nag Hammadi texts. At first, he seems to be equivalent to Archangel Michael/Prince En.lil, but because the Nag Hammadi are inverted, Sabaoth is most likely Marduk. Also, according to the same texts, Sabaoth is a Sun Archon, and Marduk is the sun god. Marduk never received Sophia's trust, of course—that was En.lil—but it looks like Marduk took over that privilege in the Gnostic texts. I don't believe there was a Jesus walking on Earth 2,000 years ago—it's most likely just a myth created by a plotting trickster god.

There is no evidence there was a feminine "Jesus" incarnated on Earth at any time, either, and I personally don't think there was. When I was told by the Orion source that "Jesus" was feminine, I am quite sure he referred to the matriarchy that came before the patriarchy. He called it "The Way of the Mother Goddess." That means we humans, at one time, even here on Earth, were well aware of the Queen of Orion as the Creatrix, and we followed the rules and the guidelines of the Universe, based on the feminine principles, so we could continue expanding the way we are designed. Then, around 2,000 years ago, En.ki and Marduk came up with the idea to hijack The Ways of the Mother Goddess and turn it to The Ways of the Father God, attempting to eliminate the matriarchy once and for all—just look at the witch hunt during the Dark Ages. Whom were the "witches" loyal to? The Father God or the Mother Goddess? I would say the latter. Thus, they were burned at the stake. Still, it seems like the truth can't be kept under wraps forever because now there is a new Mother Goddess trend.

Sophia, as the Creatrix, is obviously a part of the Gnostic texts, but in quite a derogatory fashion, where it says that matter (the material realm) was a mistake because she did not consult with her masculine counterpart before she created the Universe. There are flaws in that narrative from what I have learned.

For example, Sophia did not need a masculine counterpart to create the Universe. She had everything she needed inside herself, and nothing in her creation was a "mistake." This is something En.ki the Demiurge made up to gratify himself, representing and gratifying the masculine. The Gnostic texts are patriarchal all the way up to Source (the Monad), for whom the Gnostics use the pronoun "he." En.ki and Marduk flipped everything around, so people could worship them. Once that was done, they could set the final rules based on reward and punishment. A few centuries later, the Christian Religion was established, and even in Judaism and Islam, Jesus has a role to play, although he might not be considered the son of God but more of a prophet. All this creates a lot of loosh for the Father "God" and his son through worship and fear of God, a fear Christians are taught they must have to be dedicated Christians.

The second error in the Gnostic texts, pertaining to "Sophia's Fall," is that matter was a side product of the fall and was not part of the plan. That is obviously wrong because the material universe, comprising the developing worlds, has been a crucial part in the development of 2-UCs to become creator gods later (in many cases). All matter is condensed energy. That's not a mistake, it's the vibration of spirit energy slowed down to become what we perceive as solid, accomplished by technology.

There is still information in the Nag Hammadi texts that can be useful, but if someone wants to study them, I suggest keeping the above in mind and using your best discernment.

The Book of Revelation

I would love to rename this part of the New Testament "The Book of Deception," and we would finally hit a true chord. I have been asked if these prophecies, channeled (!) by John the Divine, are of Orion or Matrix origin. The short answer: it is of Matrix origin.

This entire deception is cleverly done by the greatest trickster god in the Universe (yes, I will give En.ki that loosh—I'm sure he likes my compliment). First, he and Marduk create the Christian Religion and set up the rules, as mentioned earlier in this chapter. Then, the two plotters plot an array of prophecies—truth in plain sight, but in a deceptive, inverted way. Marduk is now taking on the role of Archangel Michael, who will come back to fight the evils of this world, and then he will be the official King of Earth for a thousand years. It sounds a lot like the fake alien invasion.

Again, we have God as a Father figure in the Book of Revelation (REV), which is another sign of inversion, and with Marduk as Jesus, he took on the role of Michael. So, the REV is obviously a huge deception, putting religious labels to wars and upheavals they have prepared for over a millennium. It's about the Return of Jesus (Marduk), as promised in the religious texts. This pertains not only to Christianity; almost all ancient mythologies talk about a Divine Deity returning, such as Quetzalcoatl in Mesoamerica. Everybody is waiting for a returning savior. The Overlords know exactly what they are doing because we humans are hijacked, and we are waiting for our Mother to come and save us. Instead, the Big Bad Wolf is coming for The Little Red Riding Hood, i.e., us.

Project Bluebeam

Again, this entire savior scenario corresponds quite well with Project Bluebeam, which so many people have discussed over the last decades—an alien invasion that will be observed all over the world. Then, probably, the "savior" returns as Jesus, aka Marduk, who will defeat these "evil aliens" who are just holograms, inserted into the simulation in which we live. Then, Marduk will become the Glorious King of Kings (KHAN.US KHAN.UR in Sirian language).

Why all this hype? Because it's a perfect way to unite people and create a One World Government, just like President Reagan hinted at in the 1980s speech. Yes, a World Government is still on the table. There will be no more fenced-in countries, and all nations will be as one, reporting to the same World Government. Marduk himself, as the King of Kings, the KHAN.US KHAN.UR, will most likely sit on the throne of IS.RA.EL (IS for ISIS, RA for Marduk, and EL for Elohim). That's what they are preparing for in the Middle East, and that's what Hitler was planning for all along.

The Ways of the Mother Goddess in Atlantis

As mentioned in the early chapters of this book, Orion was here during the Second Construct, as well as En.ki and Marduk. Orion wanted to make sure we humans did not forget our origins. Mostly, the human soul group in those days acknowledged the Feminine Universe and a Feminine Creatrix. The main Overseer during the Atlantis Era was Prince Ninurta, who in Egypt was known as Horus the Elder. I would say that if there ever was a feminine Jesus, it was probably him, but not as a savior, but as a keeper of the Feminine "Religion," The Way of the Mother Goddess. If so, he came not to preach—it was just ongoing open communication about Divine Knowledge.

24. Attacking Orion

The Flow of Spirit Energy within the Matrix

Before we once more touch on the subject of "riding Avatars into Orion," let's start by recapping how Namlú'u Spirit Energy flows from our spirit body and all the way to our physical sapiens bodies.

Our spirit body, the "player" in the computer game, so to speak, is not in some nebulous galaxy far away—it's still within us, and always was. All En.ki and his team of geneticists did was to seduce the 3-UC—the genuine human—to play En.ki's "game." As mentioned earlier, I've had many sources convey we were seduced by sex, just like many star beings outside our current matrix are, as well, and want to come in and "try." Once we had invested our consciousness—our spirit fire—in the Matrix, En.ki made us forget. We forget who the player was and who was the avatar in the game. There was a disconnection between our spirit body and the consciousness that was, and still is, trapped here. All this happened, and happens, within us. As a metaphor, we could say the genuine 3-UC, including the spirit body, is "outside" the Matrix, and our invested spirit fire is within the Matrix. In reality, all of it is still inside us, but temporarily separated with technology, so there is very little reporting back to the spirit body. We think we *are* the false 3-UC—the Matrix mind, the astral body, and the physical body, i.e., the artificial mind, soul, and spirit body, respectively. Then there are great numbers of people who think they are only a sapiens body with a brain.

Having consciousness trapped in the Matrix is like having a finger stuck in a mouse trap. Our focus goes to the finger because that's where it hurts, and we can't stop focusing on the finger until we've removed it from the trap and made it stop hurting.

Since we got stuck in the recycling loop, the 3-UC feeds its consciousness first to a Matrix avatar, which is the astral body. From there, the energy goes to the homo sapiens sapiens body, where the spirit fires attach to the blood cells in the physical body. That's how it is now.

In Metaverse, it's going to be different. We will bypass the astral and the current astral body entirely, after they have nano-botted our sapiens bodies accordingly and created Human 4.0. They only need our *modified* sapiens bodies, the Metaverse avatar, and the spirit fire we invest, which will feed the Metaverse system and function as batteries.

From thereon, the energy goes from the modified and micro-chipped Human 4.0 into an avatar in Metaverse, which will resemble the Human 4.0 body outside Metaverse, still in this current 3-D reality. Hence, we are trapped both in an Earth body and a Metaverse body. One could say our sapiens body becomes the surrogate for the former astral body. All this is done with nanotechnology. The consciousness of all people in Metaverse is gathered within a new Grid, the Cloud, run by a supercomputer, with its "mainframe" on Mars. Now, the trapped spirit fires get stuck in Metaverse, which will be their new universe. The current Grid will be extremely weak and probably disperse and cease to exist. There are not enough people or sufficient energy to keep it up. We are already depleted of energy, and most remaining energy in the Matrix System will go into Metaverse.

Time for the Orion Attack

When it's time to attack Orion, humans in the Cloud have conformed to the will of the Overlords. As discussed earlier, the gods have already adjusted our Metaverse avatar to create a hive-mind, also strengthened by the implants in the Human 4.0 cyborgs. At first, the Overlords will let humans have a blast, as it were. There will be garments and helmets people can put on, so they can have sex in Metaverse and get the same sensations in their cyborg bodies as they have in their current Human 3.0, before Metaverse. The difference is that in Metaverse, "everything goes." All the bizarre sexual desires people have not dared to express in 3-D life they can now express in Metaverse. That is what happened in the beta version of Metaverse. The first thing some people did was to rape other avatars inside Metaverse[[83]]. So again, history repeats itself, and the Overlords lure people in with sex. Of course, as soon as Metaverse is filled with 3-UC consciousness, they can close this new trap and connect the hive-mind, modeled after what they've learned from Super Soldiers, and elsewhere. Once that is done, the Overlords can invade Orion at any time because now they can ride us—we will all be of the same mindset, i.e., the mindset of the Overlords.

Metaverse is run with nanotechnology through our cyborg sapiens bodies, so in Metaverse, we have access to Orion, aka the Nanoverse. As the Orion source said, the Overlords accomplish with technology what we humans can do without technology if we have the right training, for we are spirited. When the Invasion begins, the Overlords still need our sapiens bodies as batteries here on Earth, or it won't work. Now they can ride our Metaverse avatars into Orion. The Metaverse avatars are directly connected through our spirit bodies. Thus, we will attack our own Mother, and the Invaders will have access to our genuine Avatars through our spirit bodies. Thus, they have access to the entire Orion Universe, from the lowest regions to the highest, just like we do. They will also become creator gods, one could say, although they still use *us* as creators—they themselves can *not* create. But like ticks, they are attached to us and will benefit from our creations; particularly as they will be the minds behind anything we create.

Our spirit bodies are immortal, so regardless of what Orion does if they get invaded by a human army, the spirit bodies can't be killed or destroyed. However, the soul-mind can be destroyed, in the sense that if our spirit fire is split by energy weapons, it is very difficult to resemble them again, and they go back to the Universe as Spirit Energy. Left is only the spirit body, and we cease being human. What would happen to the spirit body after such an incident I currently do not know.

The Overlords need our soul-minds as shields (by controlling them), and our spirit bodies as vehicles in the KHAA, so they can get access to the upper regions of Orion; and later, if they win the battle, they need our spirit bodies to become creators. We don't even want to imagine what they, as creator gods, would create. One thing is obvious—it would be a tyrannical universe, ruled with iron fists. And the Overlords would continue their internal battles over power and control, with our minds in a comatose state, being their vehicles. This is not unlike what we discussed earlier in The ORION Book Volume 1, and here, about narcissism and how it works in a person on Earth: The original 3-UC is unconscious in a toddler state.

The Overlords will thus use Sophia's empathy, love, and compassion for her "children" (us) against her. En.ki apparently figures that to defeat the attacking human legion, Sophia/the Queen must kill the human souls-minds. The Overlords will be destroyed too in the process if the Queen counters in defense, but En.ki reckons that she will hesitate, and while hesitating, the Overlords can attack. Still, I think that if the Queen is completely pushed into a corner, she must destroy us in order to eliminate the Overlords. Although it would be extremely tragic, the consequences of a victorious army of Overlords are far worse.

The good news is that the Orion source seems quite confident the Overlords will not make it that far.

Think about how easy it is to control our minds completely. Look at all these young men who go to war and get killed because their President says a certain group of people are our enemies—a people no one held any grudges against until the propaganda started. These soldiers think they are patriotic. Then, when there is a ceasefire, the "enemies" are friends for a day and play cards and drink beer together. When it's time to go back to battle again, they continue killing each other. How insane is this? But few think twice about it, so we humans repeat the same patterns over and over through the millennia, and all we do when we go to war, regardless of the reason, we feed the System, and above all—the Overlords.

25. Redemption

From Immortality to Survival Mode

It's important to get some perspective on where we once were and where we are now. When we were born as 3-UCs on Tiamat, we could say we were "spirit toddlers," in lack of a better term. They put us on Tiamat to "grow up" and hopefully become a compassionate species that could contribute to the expansion of the Universe by becoming active creator gods. Now, try to imagine that back then, death was unheard of. If someone mentioned death to us then, we would not know what they were talking about. Immortality to us was the most natural thing; it could not be any other way.

Now, however, death is on our minds every day to some extent. Some people think about it all the time, in fear, while others have fleeting thoughts about it. Either way, we have gone from a state of eternal life to a state of an immense fear of death in most people. What a fall in consciousness!

The common denominator on Earth is *survival.* Everything here boils down to that "we must survive!" An eye for an eye or a tooth for a tooth, if necessary. From being a completely united soul group once, we are currently as divided as can be. And now the Overlords want us united again, but on *their* terms—the Singularity and the Cloud.

It's fear of death that keeps us trapped here, by and large. We stick to our bodies to such an extreme that if we get really sick and are in pain, we often don't even want to leave these sapiens bodies in these cases—we hang on. That's how strong the survival instinct is in our programmed bodies.

This is per design, obviously. With fear of death as a motivator, those who know more than the average human can easily manipulate us. This turns man against man and keeps us divided. Trauma keeps us bonded and alienated from each other at the same time, and there is always an inner conflict because we also inherit all our ancestors' conflicts, deeds, and misdeeds. Then we must struggle with all this and try to make sense of the world and our lives. And thus, we decline as a soul group.

Therefore, a major task is for us to conquer our fear of death to the best of our abilities. If we don't, we will forever be in the Overlords' grip. Fear of death is an implant, and we can't erase it completely, but as the saying goes, "No bravery without fear," or, "You can't be brave if you don't know fear." This is very true, so to leave the Matrix, we must not get rid of *all* fear, but we must transform fear into courage. That's the way to do it.

A New Slant on Redemption: What is it Really?

In the Wes Penre Papers, The First Level of Learning, when I was in contact with Dr. A.R. Bordon and the Life Physics Group-California (LPG-C), it soon became clear that the late Dr. Bordon wanted humankind to change in *his* way so this Matrix Experiment could keep on running. I believe his intentions were good, but he did not understand the Bigger Picture. Maybe he did at the end of his life because when I published The Second Level of Learning, he wrote to me and encouraged me to keep going. I just think that his hands were tied at that point, and he realized what a jam he had put himself in from having tried to negotiate with the Overlords directly. That he died shortly after of fast-growing pancreatic cancer is very suspicious.

The negotiation with the Overlords was, unbeknownst to Dr. Bordon, all on the Overlords' terms. Dr. Bordon wanted to negotiate for the freedom of humankind, and because Bordon put himself as an ambassador for humankind, writing a contract with him would be binding. The Overlords were merely trying, via this physics group, to get consent to what they are planning to do with us humans.

The Orion source said to me, "Did A.R. ever ask your soul group what *they* want?" By that, he meant no one can elevate themselves to be an ambassador for the human soul group without telling the same soul group about it and let them vote whether they agree to the terms. Otherwise, that person goes behind the back of the rest of us, trying to achieve something *this person* wants, without asking us. That violates freewill, and is a betrayal of trust, whether Bordon was aware of it. I, for example, do not want the same thing Dr. Bordon wanted.

From this, I want to move to the subject of redemption. This is a subject on which we all have had a misunderstanding, I think, including myself. I was confused about it until I once again reviewed some records of communication between me and the Orion source. Then it became clear that we have it all backwards! We could not understand why En.ki, for example, is redeemable after all he's done.

In fact, he is clearly redeemable, and because of that, he must *not* come to Orion. Confusing? Let me explain.

What will happen, according to my source, at the Day of Judgment, i.e., the Gnostic "Consummation of the Age," when this construct will be destroyed, and the wheats separated from the chaff, is the following: Those who are "good" will be classed as irredeemable, and those who are of the opposite will be classed as redeemable—contrary to what I thought. And there is a reason for this.

If you are irredeemable, it denotes what you have borrowed in energy throughout your existence in the Matrix will be written off, and it will be classed as you can't pay it back. We have discussed a few times that the soul is a loan, and we should pay back the loan in the form of creation and contribution to the expansion of the Universe, in one way or another. If you're irredeemable, your soul will be given to you and the energy debt will be considered repaid. Because "good people" will be of the right virtue, the Queen, and other creator gods, will trust them to balance out the energy equation, eventually, because they want a better universe for everybody.

A good comparison is if you take a bank loan. The bank lends you the money to accrue interest, so they can make a profit from what they lend you. As long as you can pay back, the loan is redeemable, but if you are in default, with no chance of paying back the loan, the loan is irredeemable, and after some years, the bank may need to write it off. Indeed, we sometimes hear that the reason banks will write off the debts is so that the person can come back to society and start producing and contributing again.

The redeemable people will be classed as those who can pay off the energy debt that they stole together with the Khan Kings. They will be ordered to pay back the loan in full—not only for the current lifetime, but for all lifetimes in this construct. If they don't have sufficient energy to do this, which they won't have, they will be left to the Khan Kings to play out the polarity "game." They will destroy each other over time, and their soul energy will return to the Cosmic Ocean; and whatever remains will be used to repair bits and pieces of the Universe. So, these people are redeemable in the sense that whatever can be retrieved from their energy will be retrieved and used to pay back the debt.

Humans must come to realization and take responsibility before the debt can be forgiven. Coming to realization and taking responsibility means refusing to go along with everything En.ki and the Khan Kings have instilled. It's much like a stranger coming to you with a packet, telling you to store it for him in your home for a while without opening it, and you agree. Then the police come and open the packet, and it's full of drugs. You will go to jail as an accomplice, because it was up to *you* not to be so naïve as to take a packet from a stranger without knowing what it contains. In other words, it's all about coming to realization and taking responsibility, no longer agreeing to the manipulation, and refusing to continue being accomplices to the Overlords' crimes. We must be willing to let go of *everything* in this construct and leave it all behind when we exit because everything here is inverted, and therefore, it is one big lie. It has to do with coming to the realization that what I just said is not an exaggeration but the truth—*everything is a lie and must be rejected by the person who leaves the Matrix.* When we can do this, we repent and stop being accomplices for hideous crimes. And thus, our debt can be forgiven. We are ready to move on and continue where we left off before the hijack of our consciousness.

For the rest, who don't come to this realization, and still prefer to remain accomplices, the time of retaliation and rectification will be short, but it can be done if a person is willing. When Orion consider some people, who are not willing to work on themselves, redeemable and unwilling to repent, whatever energy is left in that person will be retrieved by playing out polarity with the Overlords, and that person will be no more because the energy that makes up the personality will be used to pay off parts of the debt to repair the damage. But everybody will get a fair chance.

However, there is a very important caveat to all this: Being good in this sense does *not* mean giving money to someone in a system that oppresses them. It's nothing wrong with helping others in need, but that is not what we're talking about when it comes to being irredeemable. As we grow in awareness, they expect us to realize this. They are two different things—helping someone in need and becoming irredeemable. Helping someone in need only shows you *are* a good person, but there is more that needs to be done, as explained above. We must reject everything that has to do with the System and get rid of all attachments before we exit. So, in the long-term, the Queen will call back those who are "good," and the rest, who are redeemable and refuse to work on paying back, will be left to pay off the huge energy debt.

There will be those whom most of us consider "good people," but they never wake up, and they continue supporting the Overlords' System. After being given a last chance in the future, and they still dismiss their opportunity to repent, those people will be held responsible together with the Khans, and the two parties will be judged equally, because they are participants in the same crimes. Orion can't write off the debts for those who refuse to repent because they will take their stubbornness with them out into the KHAA and continue preying on the universal energy. It's time for everybody to grow up—particularly when faced with the truth, given to them by their true creators. If they still decide to keep their blinders on, it must be their choice. And believe it or not, there will be "good people" who will refuse. These people will be presented with the "bill" in a formal way. But they will not have the means to pay.

Some may argue that energy must be abundant in the Universe, so why being so firm about "loans and paybacks?"

Let's say the Queen pays back the debt for us and calls it good. What would happen? Two things would happen: 1) We come to mummy to let mummy clean up our mess, while we're hiding in her skirts like frightened children who have been naughty. The only thing we learn from that is that we do not need to be responsible because mummy will always take care of it. And 2) Other star races would consider the Queen biased toward us. Why us and not them? Eventually, "everybody" would stop making efforts, and the progress of the Universe would stagnate, and everybody gets miserable. And when the progress stagnates and star beings keep sucking in a lot of energy from the Universe for selfish purposes, giving nothing back, and Orion will become more and more depleted of useful Spirit Energy, they will start depleting other universes of energy, as well. Thus, everything will head toward destruction rather than progression.

So, the "good" people's debt will be written off because the energy is there, and they are willing to start using it constructively and for the good of all. They are irredeemable, and it will then be up to them to choose what to do and what they want.

With this new information in mind, let's return to our initial question: Is En.ki (and Marduk) redeemable? The answer is yes, and it means they are *not* welcome back into Orion. They will be judged with human accomplices who refuse to repent, and they will play out polarity in a "Hell Dimension" ("Hell" because they will create their own Hell). Eventually, they will deplete themselves and each other of all energy, and what remains will go back into the Cosmic Ocean.

What if a Bad Person was Good in a Previous Life?

This is a question I think people have asked themselves. I will take a real-life example.

A few years ago, a 21-year-old male desperado, in the middle of COVID, broke into a home where a 12-year-old girl lived. Her mother had quickly gone to the store to buy food. The desperado raped the 12-year-old, killed her, stole everything of value, and left. The Orion source asked me, "Wes, what do you think we should do with people like this?" It was an open question, and he never provided an answer. But he didn't need to. This is just something for us all to ponder because we, or representatives for the spirit group, will be summoned to an Orion Court Hearing when all this is over, and justice will be applied. Humans will be witnesses in a trial, and humankind will also be judged, so it can be sorted out who is irredeemable and who is not.

We have all lived many lifetimes in the Matrix. Depending on our upbringing, our environment, choices, coping mechanisms, and experiences in the physical world, we build a certain personality, valid for *one* lifetime only. After that, this personality is destroyed in the astral. A new astral body is created—the blueprint which resembles the new body we will be recycled into. We now have a blank slate to start all over with. Keeping this in mind, why should we judge the individual in *this* particular lifetime (such as the rapist/murderer) if he was a relatively good person in another life? We discussed this earlier, but it's important. This person should be judged as a murderer, thief, and rapist because that's who he has become in his evolution up to this point. You, who read this, are most likely none of the above. You are decent "good" people. Why are you good and not him? Because you have made more constructive choices over time than destructive choices, and that has made you into who you are today. The murderer did the same thing, although his choices were much more destructive, selfish, and evil than constructive. One could say, "Oh, it is his upbringing, so he should be forgiven. He did the best he could. He probably did better in another lifetime." Really? No, he made some horrendous choices to become who he is now, and he should be judged as that person. Moreover, if we forgive him and let him out in the KHAA, we let a murderer and rapist out to roam freely in Orion. We don't want that. It's my conclusion that people, such as this guy, will be judged together with the Overlords, and one day, he will play out polarity and return to the Ocean. In that sense, one could perhaps say that his karma played out in the end, after all.

26. The Importance of Philosophy

Philosophy is more important than anything else if we want to learn something about ourselves, the Matrix, and particularly the realm outside the construct.

By saying that, we are back full circle because this is also how I started this book and the book before that. However, before we apply philosophy to figure out things for real, we need a foundation, i.e., we need a knowledge base to build upon. We must have some basic knowledge about the Matrix, the Overlords, and the Agenda, so we can continue our journey from there, which *must* be philosophical in nature. If we do not transform our curiosity and thirst for truth from information seeking on the Internet, in books, and elsewhere, into philosophy, which is the knowledge of the higher mind, we will all stagnate and go round in circles, which many people do.

The search for truth often starts when a person, often because of trauma, realizes there must be more to existence than what we experience in this earthly and very physical realm. Thus, the journey begins. For a long time, we are like sponges—we want to know *everything* about *everything*, and we deep-dive into any and all archives and information we can find. Our thirst for knowledge seems endless, and the more we drink, the thirstier we get. This is good; we learn a lot. In the beginning, we might absorb much disinformation mixed with some fundamental truths, but most of us learn over time to better distinguish between the two.

However, one day we come to a turning point. We realize that for some time we have gone round in circles, and we are stagnating, recycling the same topics and the same information in different packages repeatedly, without learning much that is new, and it feels frustrating. We are not getting anywhere anymore, and we feel almost desperate, or at least tired, and perhaps even burned out from all this research. Although we have learned a lot, we intuitively know there is more to learn. But regardless of how many books we read, how many YouTube channels we watch, and how much research we do, by studying other people's research, we get no further.

If not before then, this is when we must substitute truth-seeking in the outside world for philosophy. We realize that the truth is not "out there" but "in here." The truth is inside all of us, and each one of us; it's *not* outside. The outside is always distorted because it's a mix of our collective conclusions, illusions, half-truths, manipulation, and what have you. The only truth you will ever know must come from inside.

Philosophers often encounter a common theme. Those who are not yet at the point in their evolution to apply philosophy to their truth-seeking efforts cry and scream for "evidence" and "proof." They accuse the philosopher to imagine things as if that would be a bad thing, and they need to see physical proof of the philosopher's conclusions. This nonsense, the philosopher must reject and instead continue his introspection. The entire idea of philosophy is that it expands *beyond* the physical realm of scientific "evidence," which later proves to be flawed, anyway, and is always prone to change.

The evidence and proof, so much cried for by those who oppose the philosopher, is only valid within the physical world, the Matrix, at best. Philosophy expands further into the Spiritual World, and that's where we must look because that's where we originate. We were never physical beings to begin with; the physical world was posed upon us by physical beings who had no clue what Spirit was. Therefore, they must drag us down into the physical realm to eat us and control us. Once here, we are dealing with savages, and over time, a large portion of the human population has become savages, too. Those who relentlessly cry for evidence and proof of the philosopher's conclusions and hypotheses are doing the same thing the Overlords do because humans who desperately attack the philosopher in such a way don't understand Spirit, either. There is no time, and there is no use trying to "educate" these people because they will not listen to what you have to say, mostly because they don't, and sometimes never will, understand it. They might simply lack Spirit.

We are all, foremost, responsible for our own evolution, and so are the critics of the philosopher. Therefore, let it remain so. Let the philosopher philosophize and the critic blindly criticize. The two are on different paths. That's all there is to it. Still, paths can change.

There is very little that is new under the sun. Increasing our awareness and consciousness is usually not a matter of finding out something new that will elevate us to some higher dimension. It's a matter of remembering what we already know, but that has been occluded and denied to us for a very long time by those who don't have our best interest in mind. Therefore, if what we do is "evolving" to a state at which we already once were, how can we do this by only looking for answers in the physical realm? That would obviously not work. Thus, we would end up running around in circles.

Hence, philosophy is senior to anything you can learn in the physical realm. So, let's ponder, deep-think, and most importantly, discuss our thoughts with others (but they must be like-minded, or it will have the opposite effect). Let us do this, and it will soon take us to a whole new level of understanding.

I hope this book has been helpful, and I wish you all the best on your journey from here on out. And I usually end off with this:

I'll see you on the other side of the Grid!

Wes Penre, June 28, 2023

Appendix: How to Exit Through the Grid

Over the years, I have written multiple articles and made videos on how to exit the Matrix through a hole in the Grid that En.ki set up around Earth at the beginning of the Matrix. You can still find them on my blog at wespenrevideo.com in the "Exiting the Grid" section.

I started by giving simple instructions because it is essentially easy to exit. However, I noticed people must have thought it seemed *too* simple, so they complicated things, and all the *what ifs* came into the picture, and they just escalated because of people's fear of the unknown. It's understandable to fear the unknown, but this fear must be transformed into courage and overridden to where bravery is stronger than fear, or the exit will obviously not happen, and the person will fall into the recycling trap again.

This chapter will most likely be the last I write on how to exit through the Grid after physical death to leave the Matrix for good. I will end this topic where I once started by explaining it plainly and simply. Please don't overthink it, or you will become your own obstacle, giving into your fear and miss out. Make the exit plan swift and simple. Learn to build confidence.

If you truly want to exit, please continue reading. This is required:

1. You must get rid of fears until you get to where you know you will succeed. You accomplish this by doing *inner work*. You will know when you are ready enough to override the fears—you will feel it. Make *very* sure you remove abusive people from your immediate life, or it will be very difficult to build the courage.

1. For me, at least, as a healing program, the *21-Day Reprogramming* has worked excellently.[84] It also helps if you have a trustworthy person in your life with whom you can have safe, completely open, non-judgmental communication and that person can be open with you. There is no faster healing than that–better even than the best therapy with the best therapist (this claim comes not from me but from a professor in psychology, Sam Vaknin, and I know firsthand he is correct).

1. Make very sure that when you die, you have no attachments to the Matrix, and you are ready to leave everything behind. Don't be lazy with this one. Attachments include but are not restricted to, friends, relatives, significant others, pets, Matrix life itself, the Overlords, and material things alike. The bottom line is this: Make sure you can leave without having second thoughts because you feel you will miss something so much that you will hesitate when you enter the astral plane.

That is what you need to work on while you are still living this current life on Earth. If you truly feel you have already accomplished these three steps, congratulations! Then you will read this article without doubting yourself when exiting–at least not more than you know you can handle when the day of exit comes.

The Exit Strategy

Here is a simple exit strategy, the one and only I will use. If you don't see any updates to this on my blog in the future (wespenrevideos.com), the following will be the workable technique I will use–nothing more, nothing less:

1. When I die, I will look "up" in relation to my deceased human body, and I will spot the Grid above me (a fuzzy net surrounding the Earth, having holes in it).
2. I spot one of the many holes in the Grid and I think along these lines, "I am through a hole in the Grid NOW!" The astral is immediately thought-responsive, so my thoughts will execute instantly. Therefore, the word NOW! is very important, or you create your own delay.

1. Once out of the Grid, I will immediately think, "I am at the Orion Queen's Highest possible aspect NOW!" I will be there in an instant, regardless of where she roams at that moment.

That's it.

The only couple of things I want to add is that if you encounter somebody, no matter who, when you are in the astral, PAY NO ATTENTION to them at all. They can appear as angels, spirit guides, false dead relatives, and even a false Jesus, or a tunnel of light—don't go there, as it leads to the recycling center, and you'll be trapped in a Matrix body again with full amnesia (shapeshifting is the norm rather than a rarity in the astral). Whatever it might be, wishing to distract you, *FOCUS on your task to leave*, and no one will be able to stop you. To be stopped, you must *agree* to be stopped. *No one can stop a pure intention and a strict focus*. The other thing is, if you feel lost in the astral for any reason, just start over: "I am at a hole in the Grid NOW!" and you'll be there. Then repeat 1-3. If things seem foggy or cloudy, think, "CLARITY NOW!" and you'll get clarity.

This is all there is to it.

About Other Ways to Exit

As mentioned, many people think the above process sounds too simple, and it might scare them and make them doubt it's that easy. They want to be on the "safe side."

A friend of mine released a paper he called, *Exit Handout (Steps to Leave the Matrix),* which the reader can find on my blog.[[85]] It has become very popular since it was released, which means many people appreciate a more detailed procedure to exit than what I just gave you. That is perfectly fine with me; I am not concerned about *how* people exit through the Grid, so long as they exit. If it feels safer to have more "meat" to the procedure, this handout is for you, and it's well written.

There are researchers on the Internet (and you can find some information in different books, too), instructing people how to leave the Matrix. I have checked out many of these alternative procedures, but based on the knowledge I have, none of them will help you leave the Matrix. Unless I have missed some alternatives, there is no other way, in my opinion, than to follow the above procedure and just go. The truth is often simple—don't look for alternatives that are too complicated. They will most likely not work. And why would we choose a more complicated exit when the hole-in-the-Grid plan is so straight forward? My take on it is that even if someone finds an alternative route, I will stick to a hole in the Grid. I have a difficult time imagining a quicker and simpler route out of here.

I wish you a great journey through the rest of your life here in the Matrix, and I hope to see you on the other side, in the Greater Universe (Orion), as a true creator god, away from the Matrix oppression, trauma, and misery. I am sure that we who choose to exit will meet in Orion. I think we need each other there, and those who exit first may wait for more of us to arrive. Then we can have a blast. I think that's something exciting to look forward to. So, hang in there, try to find things you enjoy doing, while still in your sapiens body, and do your best to enjoy the time you have left here. After all, it's mind over matter, so let's be creative and learn how to enjoy our current existence. It's so easy to give into Evil and just think everything is bad. It is, but only if we, in our minds, make it so.

Index

1

2

3

4

9

A

B

C

D

dimensions, 1, 15, 17, 27, 28, 30, 64, 78, 115, 116, 117, 162, 163, 166, 176, 186, 200, 220, 223

Direct Current, 162

Divine message, 245

DNA, 7, 40, 41, 42, 43, 47, 50, 70, 95, 110, 122, 214, 215, 217, 222, 223, 234, 237, 238

Dome, 47, 71, 112, 145, 191, 194, 196

doppelgängers, 145

double terminated, 182

Dracos, 77, 79, 145

Drinking blood, 201

E

Earth, 1, 2, 3, 4, 5, 6, 16, 21, 23, 26, 27, 28, 30, 31, 32, 33, 34, 35, 36, 37, 38, 39, 42, 44, 46, 47, 48, 50, 52, 53, 57, 63, 69, 70, 71, 74, 77, 78, 79, 80, 81, 82, 83, 87, 89, 116, 119, 120, 122, 124, 130, 131, 134, 136, 139, 140, 141, 142, 158, 159, 161, 165, 166, 178, 182, 183, 187, 192, 194, 195, 196, 199, 200, 214, 232, 236, 239, 245, 246, 248, 253, 254, 255, 257, 272, 274

Earth is a school, 2

Earthbound Beings, 1

Eddas, 76

egg, 16, 63

Egypt, 6, 23, 36, 39, 76, 82, 250

Eisenhower, 109, 110

EL, 249

electrical fence, 234

electromagnetic spectrum, 27, 165

F

G

H

I

L

N

O

P

Q

S

T

U

Y

Yaldabaoth, 48

Z

[[1]] The Seven Hermetic Principles: Video Advice YouTube channel: "Very few know this" | Ex-Occultist Shares Hidden Knowledge

[[2]] https://thepeoplesvoice.tv/wef-orders-govts-to-arrest-citizens-who-read-fake-news-online/

[[3]] https://en.wikipedia.org/wiki/You%27ll_own_nothing_and_be_happy#Background

[[4]] https://nypost.com/2023/04/15/activist-warns-of-global-push-adding-bugs-to-the-menu/

[[5]] https://wespenre.com

[[6]] See "The ORION Book" (vol. 1) for a better understanding of who Sophia, aka *the Orion Queen*, the Creatrix of our universe, is.

[[7]] Research and read the Egyptian Osiris-Isis-Horus story, also discussed in the WPP.

[[8]] This list, here in an edited version, was also included in the WPP, but we need to be reminded, and it's helpful to include it when studying the material in this Orion series.

[[9]] See the Wes Penre Papers (WPP) for more information.

[[10]] *Ibid.*

[[11]] https://en.wikipedia.org/wiki/Hamites

[[12]] https://en.wikipedia.org/wiki/Semitic_people

[[13]] https://en.wikipedia.org/wiki/Japhetites

[[14]] See The Wes Penre Papers, The Fourth Level of Learning: "The Rigel War."

[[15]] https://en.wikipedia.org/wiki/Aeon_(Gnosticism)

[[16]] https://en.wikipedia.org/wiki/Pleroma#Gnosticism/

[[17]] My term for the Spirit Universe, i.e., the nano world or nano universe.

[[18]] 3-UC means "Three Unit Composite," i.e., soul + mind + spirit body.

[[19]] https://www.crystalinks.com/emerald.html

[[20]] https://wespenre.com/2019/02/03/fourth-level-of-learning-paper-7-the-solar-war/

[[21]] https://www.greekmythology.com/Myths/The_Myths/Titanomachy/titanomachy.html

[[22]] https://www.worldhistory.org/article/225/enuma-elish—-the-babylonian-epic-of-creation—-fu/

[[23]] See The Enûma Eliš.

[[24]] From here on out, I want to distinguish between *spirit group* and *soul group*. We humans are spirited, and we don't function the same way as the soul groups in the physical realms. We human did not become a soul group until we were tricked into the Matrix.

[[25]] "Water planet" doesn't mean it was made up of oceans. It means it existed in the Cosmic Waters, i.e., the KHAA, i.e., the Spirit Universe.

[[26]] https://www.amazon.com/Ra-Material-Ancient-Astronaut-Speaks/dp/089865260X

[[27]] https://www.youtube.com/watch?v=reXZwL_2Aag

[[28]] https://wespenre.com/2019/02/03/fourth-level-of-learning-paper-5-lucifers-rebellion/

[[29]] I will use Avatar with a capital "A" when discussing our 3-UC Avatar, and I will use avatar with a small "a" when discussing En.ki's artificial soul.

[[30]] Regarding introjects vs. the outer world, see *The ORION Book, Volume 1, Chapter 9: Adopting the Narcissist's Mind*, p. 192ff.

[[31]] Merriam-Webster, "Pleroma."

[[32]] *Ibid. op. cit.*

[[33]] https://wespenre.com/2019/01/30/second-level-of-learning-paper-2-creation-of-universes/

[[34]] Sitchin, *The War of Gods and Men*, https://www.amazon.com/Wars-God-Men-Zecharia-Sitchin/dp/B000Z4OCMI

[[35]] https://en.wikipedia.org/wiki/Walk-in_(concept)

[[36]] See Chapter 1 for more info about the bloodlines of the gods.

[[37]] Read more about this program in the Wes Penre Papers, The First level of Learning at wespenre.com.

[[38]] ©1982. Can be ordered from Amazon.

[[39]] This is also a term the now 100 years old Henry Kissinger coined about soldiers.

[[40]] https://en.wikipedia.org/wiki/Operation_Paperclip

[[41]] YouTube: "How Britain and America Inspired Nazi Eugenics" https://www.youtube.com/watch?v=7Dyyt2kVOEg

[[42]] *Ibid.*

[[43]] Pronounced *Orshitch.*

[[44]] https://www.ancestry.com/. Search *María Marija Orsic Oršić Ortisch Orschitsch*

[[45]] *Ibid.*

[[46]] https://en.wikipedia.org/wiki/Nazi_UFOs

[[47]] Scale-Models.co.uk: "Squadron Haunebu II - the troublesome build - being finished..."

[[48]] https://en.wikipedia.org/wiki/Thule_Society

[[49]] https://en.wikipedia.org/wiki/Thule_Society#Beliefs

[[50]] *Ibid.*

[[51]] https://www.washingtonpost.com/archive/lifestyle/2004/02/19/ike-and-the-alien-ambassadors/4698e544-1dc8-4573-8b8d-2b48d2a6305e/

[[52]] https://wingmakers.com/

[[53]] https://wespenrevideos.com, *Wes Penre: Video 263: Needs, Trauma, Behavior, and Reprogramming.*

[[54]] Available at amazon.com. Type in "Michael Newton books."

[[55]] See Professor Sam Vaknin's YouTube channel for much more information on all this.

[[56]] Apparently, they consider the Fourth Dimension being Time, and thus, they skip it and go to the Fifth instead.

[[57]] *Magick* with a "k" is a term coined by the magician Aleister Crowley to distinguish between ritual magic and stage magic.

[[58]] Wes Penre, June 15, 2012: The Second Level of Learning, Paper 2: *The Creation of Universes*, subsection 2: *A New Way of Looking at the Structure of the Omniverse from an Interdimensional Perspective.*

[[59]] Regarding the nano-second and the alignment with the Galactic Center, see "The Wes Penre Paper, The First Level of Learning," where this is discussed in great detail.

[[60]] Ref., *Harald Kautz Vella on Transhumanism, AI, sentient world simulation, targeted individuals, dark arts, demons (July, 2021)* [circa 10 mins. into the video].

[[61]] Ref., Winter Watch: *Understanding and Countering Sentient World Simulation.*

[62] Updated information: In "The ORION Book," vol. 1, I wrote we are irredeemable if we don't repent, which is how we humans like to think about it. After reviewing old conversations with my Contact, I noticed that Orion considers it the other way around: Def. of redeem: "[to] gain or regain possession of (something) in exchange for payment: "Statutes enabled state peasants to redeem their land."" So, if a person owes something, they usually have to pay. Let's say they refuse to pay or can't pay; they could have their land redeemed.

If a person does *not* want to repent, i.e., letting go of everything Khan King-related, they still owe the energy debt and have to pay, and their spiritual energy will eventually be redeemed (withdrawn). They are still redeemable.

If another person wants to repent, the debt is "written off," even though the person owes it, and Orion will not redeem their spirit energy because we will be able to "pay back" while living in Orion where we contribute with our energy to the Orion community.

[[63]] Go to TikTok and search for, "billy carson multiverse" The first that shows up is, "Does the #multiverse exist?"

[[64]] Just when I was about to publish this book, I was notified about the following evidence, a report released by the U.S. Army, proving what I've said all along: https://wespenrevideos.com/2023/06/30/cyborg-soldier-2050-human-machine-fusion-and-the-implications-for-the-future-of-the-dod/

[[65]] On YouTube, search for, "Super Soldier Talk – Penny Bradley – SSP Dark Fleet Pilot"

[[66]] https://www.youtube.com/watch?v=JuE8eZunozc

[[67]] Reuters, May 11, 2023: "Fact Check-Quote 'children must have sexual partners' falsely attributed to the UN"

[[68]] Medical News Today: "Sex and sexual health tips for transgender women after gender-affirming surgery" among other studies.

[[69]] https://www.insidephilanthropy.com/

[[70]] YouTube: ""Why Is Nobody Paying Attention To This..." | Jordan Peterson" https://www.youtube.com/watch?v=CQ_2V59urj4

[[71]] Amazon.com: "Synthetic Super Intelligence and the Transmutation of Humankind: A Roadmap to the Singularity and Beyond."

[[72]] I sometimes use the term "gods," not because they are gods, but because that's how they see themselves.

[[73]] University of Surrey, 22 February 2021: "A new study reveals that quantum physics can cause mutations in our DNA"

[[74]] *Ibid. op cit.*

[[75]] Wikipedia: "Synthetic Environment for Analysis and Simulations"

[[76]] It should here be added that the word "simulation" does not imply it's not real—it's as real as the human mind makes it. Compare this to the Matrix we live in, which is also a simulation. However, to us it's real. Therefore, Orion could be considered a simulation, too, very real to those who roam there.

[[77]] Medium.com: "Sentient World Simulation: You're In It Now"

[[78]] *Ibid. op. cit.*

[[79]] Cointelegraph, May 5, 2015: "US Govt Develops a Matrix-Like World Simulating the Virtual You"

[[80]] This book can be purchased at Amazon.com.

[[81]] "Patrix" is another term for Matrix. The former emphasizes we live in a patriarchal "matrix." The term Matrix refers to the feminine, as in "Ma."

[[82]] This narrative was originally posted on my forum at *wespenreboards.com*. Signing up is free.

[[83]] See Sam Vaknin's YouTube channel.

[[84]] https://wespenrevideos.com/wp-content/uploads/2021/07/Video-263-Needs-Trauma-Behavior-and-Reprogramming.pdf

[[85]] https://wespenrevideos.com/2022/07/21/exit-handout-steps-to-leave-the-matrix/ [1]

---

1.   https://wespenrevideos.com/2022/07/21/exit-handout-steps-to-leave-the-matrix/